The New York Times

GUIDE
TO COIN
COLLECTING

𝕿𝖍𝖊 𝕹𝖊𝖜 𝖄𝖔𝖗𝖐 𝕿𝖎𝖒𝖊𝖘

GUIDE
TO COIN
COLLECTING

Ed Reiter

Foreword by Scott A. Travers

St. Martin's Griffin 🙢 New York

www.stmartins.com

Design by Michael Mendelsohn

ISBN 0-312-29126-4

First Edition: August 2002

10 9 8 7 6 5 4 3 2 1

To Patt

Contents

Acknowledgments

Coin collecting is the greatest hobby in the world, and *The New York Times* is the greatest newspaper in the world. That's why I derived such pleasure and pride from writing the Numismatics column in the Sunday edition of *The Times* each and every week for nearly a decade, from July 1, 1979, to January 15, 1989. And that's why I'm so pleased and proud to be reunited with *The Times* through this book. During a career in journalism that spans more than 40 years, I have written thousands of newspaper and magazine articles about coins and coin collecting—including nearly 500 columns in *The Times*. I also have edited numerous books. But this is the first time I've written a book myself. It has been a labor of love—with plenty of labor in that mix.

The labor it took to give birth to this book was made much easier by the generous assistance of many people. I want to express my deep appreciation to the following:

John Albanese, David T. Alexander, Harlan J. Berk, Steve Blum, Stephen Bobbitt, Q. David Bowers, John Dannreuther, Beth Deisher, Thomas K. DeLorey, Stella M. Domski, David L. Ganz, Kathy Ganz, Marcy Gibbel, Barbara Gregory, David Hall, David C. Harper, John Iddings, Jay W. Johnson, R. W. Julian, Chris Karstedt, Matt Kilbourne, Mike Levitas, Chester L. Krause, James F. Lowney, Sharon McPike, James L. Miller, Clifford L. Mishler, Rick Montgomery, Donn Pearlman, Jennifer Reiter, Edward C. Rochette, Maurice Rosen, Tim Scudder, Diana Sedgwick, Michael Sedgwick, Jeffery R. Shoop, Kari Stone, Barbara Travers, Harvey C. Travers, Scott A. Travers and Fred Weinberg.

I owe special thanks to those who helped me put together photographs. These include the American Numismatic Association, Amos Press/Coin World, Bowers and Merena Galleries, the British Royal Mint, Krause Publications, Miller Magazines, the Professional Coin Grading Service, Scott Travers Rare Coin Galleries Inc., the United States Mint and, individually, Harlan J. Berk, Steve Bobbitt, David and Kathy Ganz, R. W. Julian and Fred Weinberg. Bob Julian also provided tremendous support and assistance by reviewing important sections of the book for historical accuracy, drawing upon his knowledge as one of the nation's greatest numismatic researchers and scholars. Several individuals granted me long and important interviews on subjects that figure prominently in the book and about which they are experts. Among these were John Albanese on grading, Steve Blum on bullion coins, Fred Weinberg on mint errors, and Jay Johnson on the operations of the United States Mint, of which he is a former director.

My wife Patt and five children (Jennifer, Caroline, Christopher, Timothy and Allison) gave me needed time and space to work on this project with minimum interruption—most of the time, anyway.

Mike Levitas of The Times played a pivotal role by inviting me to undertake this project in the first place. He also provided occasional prodding, which was highly effective and no doubt necessary. When it comes to prodding, he, too, is an expert.

Last, but far from least, I am forever indebted to Scott A. Travers, who not only served as my agent on this project but also made innumerable contributions to enhancing the contents of the book. Having written numerous coin books himself (several of which I edited), Scott had been down this road before—and he made my journey far easier than it would have been without his astute guidance. Among his most valuable contributions is his insightful analysis of coin grading, a subject on which he is a leading authority.

Foreword

Coin collecting provides an unparalleled journey into the fields of art, culture, history and finance. It provides a window on our world that allows us to view people and their civilizations.

Gaining the fullest appreciation of the sometimes complicated trip that is *numismatics*—the study of coins, paper money and medallic art—requires an understandable introduction and a grand tour.

The New York Times Guide to Coin Collecting serves as the best introduction available with the grandest tour guide of all. It is a landmark, milestone work—the finest, most significant introduction to the land of coin collecting ever authored.

Visitors to Coinland can find no better personal tour guide than Ed Reiter. For nearly a decade, he served as Numismatics columnist for America's most prestigious newspaper, *The New York Times*. He used this bully pulpit to report on events in the realm of coins, analyze trends and promote the hobby's interests through this weekly column. In the process, he established himself as the nation's savviest and most gifted numismatic journalist. Ed Reiter has been a career journalist for more than 40 years, and a writer and columnist on numismatic subjects for more than 30 years.

The New York Times Guide to Coin Collecting reflects and incorporates the literary talents of this exceptionally skilled author, whose understanding of both the fun and complexity of coin collecting greatly assists the reader.

From the birth of coins in the seventh century B.C. to the advent of the certified coin in 1986—from early copper "large cents" to late-date Lincoln cents—and from horse-powered screw presses to modern mint technology, Ed Reiter combines his unique historical perspective with the most relevant facts of the here-and-now.

This wonderful read—an almost seamless transition between yesteryear and today—gives the reader the mindset necessary to make informed purchases, while still understanding and appreciating coinage as an artisan's crafted work. Ed Reiter maintains his hold on the science of coins and the mechanics of everything from grading to online auctions, but he never loses sight of coins as objects of art.

Coins are history in your hands, and *The New York Times Guide to Coin Collecting* in your hands can be the wonderful beginning of a lifelong interest in coins and everything they have to offer.

—Scott A. Travers

Introduction

"Numismatics." Most people can't even pronounce it, much less define it. To those who become familiar with it, though, it's a word with extremely special meaning—a four-syllable term for a four-star hobby, for numismatics is another way of saying "coin collecting."

Coins have appealed to man's collecting instincts ever since the very first ones were struck in Asia Minor more than 500 years before the birth of Christ. They're handheld works of art. They're miniature milestones along the march of time. Many times, they're stores of precious metal. Often, they're worth far more than face value—and far more than just their metal content—as collectibles. Saving them can be an exceptional investment, and best of all, collecting them can be tremendous fun.

In a way, collecting coins provides the same kind of fun, and sometimes the same kind of profit, as digging up buried treasure. The treasure isn't hidden in the ground, and tracking it down doesn't require a map, but still there's a sense of adventure, an air of excitement—and ultimately, a thrill of discovery—in locating coins that are needed to finish a set. For those who buy wisely and well, there's also an ultimate payoff, for collecting rare coins, like searching for buried treasure, has the potential to be a richly rewarding pursuit. Along the way, those who pursue this pastime often form enduring friendships with others who share their interest as they congregate at shows and join and participate in clubs.

Coin collecting today is among the most popular hobbies in the world. Its popularity has soared in the United States since 1999, when the United States Mint began producing special quarter dollars honoring the 50 states of the Union. This "statehood quarter" program is less than half finished as these words are being written; it is scheduled to continue for a full 10 years, through the end of 2008. Even non-collectors are looking for these distinctive Washington quarters; in fact, the U.S. Mint estimates that perhaps 120 million Americans are seeking and saving the coins. This is stirring unprecedented interest in the coin collecting hobby as a whole, and creating more excitement in the field than it ever enjoyed before.

Most collectors in the United States confine their collecting to U.S. coinage, but many use a far broader frame of reference, in terms of both time and area—collecting coins from earlier periods of history, all the way back to ancient times, and hundreds of other countries around the globe.

For more than 25 centuries, coins have been interwoven with the history of mankind. They have expressed the aspirations and achievements of the nations that produced them, mirrored the cultures of the peoples that utilized them—and ultimately, endured as permanent mementos and lasting legacies after those nations and cultures faded away.

By their nature, coins possess greater permanence than almost any other products of human endeavor. Coins of ancient Greece and Rome linger to this day as links to those long-dead civilizations, centuries after more massive and grandiose monuments have crumbled and turned to dust.

This book will take readers back to the beginning of coins as primitive objects, and then move forward through the ages of human history and the stages of coins' development as collectibles. It will concentrate on coinage of the United States, and coin collecting's expansion in this country, because that is the focus of interest and activity for most American practitioners of this "king of hobbies."

In recent years, the base of traditional collectors has been broadened substantially by newcomers to the marketplace who think of themselves not as hobbyists, but rather as "investors." Often, this new breed of buyer finds the hobby's lure irresistible and crosses over the line to become a collector.

Even for those who don't save coins at all, as either collectibles or investments, the subject has the appeal of a "spectator sport"— for money, after all, concerns and interests everyone.

I have sought to make this guided tour through the wonderful world of coin collecting one that will catch the fancy—and hold the attention—of all who read it, whether they are collectors, investors or merely spectators. That is the same approach I used during nearly a decade as Numismatics columnist for the Sunday *New York Times*. Now, as then, I am striving to reach not just hobby insiders but everyone who finds money interesting—particularly interesting money.

The tour is about to start, so pull up a comfortable chair and join me as we begin *The New York Times Guide to Coin Collecting*.

𝔗𝔥𝔢 𝔑𝔢𝔴 𝔜𝔬𝔯𝔨 𝔗𝔦𝔪𝔢𝔰

GUIDE
TO COIN
COLLECTING

....

Chapter 1

The Fascination of Coins

....

Through most of recorded history, money has been a preoccupation, a pursuit—even a passion—for much of the human race. People have devoted endless hours to earning it, winning it, amassing it, hoarding it, counting it, investing it, protecting it and worrying whether they'll ever have enough of it.

For one particular group of people, money holds special appeal not as a medium of exchange or even a store of value, but rather as an object to be admired in and of itself. These people are called *numismatists*—a fancy term that simply means they study and collect various forms of money, especially coins. In short, they are coin collectors.

Coin collectors come in all ages, nationalities, social and economic strata, income levels and degrees of coin-related knowledge and sophistication. They range from youngsters plucking shiny cents from ordinary pocket change to wealthy investors assembling portfolios of rare and expensive gold coins. Nowadays their ranks can be measured in the millions: Based on a survey conducted in early 2000, the United States Mint concluded that more than 120 million Americans were setting aside its special 25-cent pieces commemorating the 50 states of the Union. That's nearly one-half of the entire population of the country. Most of those people undoubtedly were dabblers, rather than serious collectors. Still, their expression of interest in the 50 State Quarters Program, as the Mint has dubbed it, reflected the appeal that coins—and coin collecting—can hold for even people who aren't confirmed collectors.

That's a far cry from the way things were in earlier periods of history, and even a hundred years ago in the United States. For that matter, there was a time when coins didn't even exist.

▶ The Origin of Coinage

Coinage was born in Asia Minor, more than six centuries before the birth of Christ and just a few hundred miles away from Bethlehem. It is generally accepted that the first coins were struck in Lydia, a kingdom located along the Aegean Sea in what today is part of western Turkey. Archaeologists place the date at about 640 B.C., during the reign of King Ardys.

Great cultures had flourished before that time. Egypt, Babylonia, Assyria—all had shone brightly before their glory faded, and all had left tangible evidence of their grandeur in the form of exquisite jewelry, finely engraved obelisks and other works that flaunted both their wealth and the craftsmanship of their artisans. In none of those lands, however, has evidence ever surfaced that they produced coins in the days when they bestrode the ancient world.

There, as elsewhere, barter was the system by which ordinary people obtained goods and services, just as they had done since the dawn of time. Tools and weapons might be exchanged for cattle, food for clothing or labor for linen. Men of wealth and power devised a more elaborate way to measure the relative value of gems and precious metals: They used special weights made of base metal or stone as standards of exchange. These came in varying sizes and typically were made in the shape of animals—bronze lions and stone ducks, for example.

When Lydia rose briefly to preeminence in the region as a

thriving commercial center, its merchants felt the need for a simpler means of exchange that would reassure all parties while also facilitating trade. They hit upon the idea of having the king issue small ingots impressed with a standard design as units of set value in business transactions. These were the first objects to satisfy the basic definition of a *coin*: a piece of metal with a distinctive stamp and fixed value and weight, issued by a government as money.

Electrum stater of Lydia. This is among the earliest coins ever made.
Photos courtesy R. W. Julian.

The earliest coins were made from *electrum*, an alloy of gold and silver found naturally and abundantly in and around the Lydian capital of Sardis. The bean-shaped ingots were punched on one side with a rudimentary design, while the other side bore striations imparted by the roughened face of the anvil when the coiner hammered the die into the metal.

Lydian coins became more elaborate in time, bearing designs on both sides showing familiar images such as the likeness of a lion. It remained for the Greeks, however, to elevate coins from merely utilitarian tools of trade to breathtaking works of art. Greek city-states were quick to follow Lydia's lead, and by the fifth century B.C. their coinage was displaying intricate, masterful designs. Gods and goddesses, human figures, plants, animals—all held sway on stunning Greek coins in glorious high relief. Not surprisingly, ancient Greek coinage has been avidly pursued by coin connoisseurs ever since. Caesar Augustus, for instance, is known to have given beautiful Greek coins to friends on special occasions.

Athenian tetradrachm. One of the greatest coins of ancient Greece.
Photos courtesy Harlan J. Berk.

Roman coinage lacked the elegance and beauty of its Greek antecedents. It compensated for this with far greater diversity. Roman coins were issued in so many different varieties, and with such frequency, that they served as a running metallic account of major—and even everyday—events in Roman history. They did so in a way that was brutally honest, often portraying their subjects—notably Roman rulers—in ways that might charitably be described as extremely unflattering.

▶ Coins as Collectibles

As centuries passed, the practice of issuing coins took root around the world. Barter continued to play an important role in underdeveloped areas and in times of economic stagnation. By the year 1000, however, most of the civilized world had access to coinage of some sort and it was used extensively.

Less visibly and more gradually, small numbers of people began to set aside examples of coinage that intrigued them, and to study the circumstances surrounding their origin and usage. The aspects that attracted them were much the same as those that make coins compelling to numismatists today:

Syracusan dekadrachm. Considered one of the most beautiful coins of all time. *Photos courtesy Harlan J. Berk.*

- ▶ **Beauty** Many coins possess extraordinary elegance. Greek coins, in particular, are miniature works of art, and owning them can be a source of tremendous pride and satisfaction, not unlike the sense of exhilaration that comes from owning graceful Grecian urns or marble busts.
- ▶ **Historic significance.** Coins are like mileposts along the highway of civilization, conveying a sense of what and who were important at a given time and place. Roman coins, especially, give their owners the feeling that they are holding history in their hands. This feeling is heightened with coins that can be linked to specific historic events, such as, the Roman denarius depicting the Ides of March conspiracy to assassinate Julius Caesar, and the 30 pieces of silver—Greek imperial tetradrachms—for which the apostle Judas betrayed Christ.
- ▶ **Diversity.** Coins can be collected in many different ways—by country of origin, historical period, subject matter, size and shape, metallic composition and even by the artist who designed them and the mint where they were made.

Ides of March denarius. Brutus appears on this Roman coin recalling his role in assassinating Julius Caesar. *Photos courtesy Harlan J. Berk.*

▶ **Durability.** Coins are among the most enduring artifacts handed down through the ages. In many cases, they provide the best available portraits—perhaps the *only* portraits—of ancient rulers. Though the majestic temples and large works of art produced under those rulers have long since disappeared or lie in ruins, many coins survive—sometimes in flawless condition—as testaments to their attainments.

▶ **Portability.** Unlike urns and marble busts or, for that matter, Great Masters' paintings, coins can be easily stored and transported. Thus, an exhibition of these handheld artworks can be easily arranged—even if the "viewing" is just a private showing for their owner.

▶ **Rarity and value.** These may not have been as apparent and important to the earliest collectors of coins, aside from the intrinsic value precious-metal coins enjoyed, but modern-day numismatists—drawing upon knowledge gleaned from long and thorough research—have established the relative rarity of coins from different eras, countries and mints. Some are exceedingly rare, even unique, and these command premiums rivaling those of major works of art.

Until modern times, interest in collecting coins was limited for the most part to aristocrats, scholars, high church officials and wealthy merchants—in other words, people who possessed the leisure time or the wherewithal or both to indulge such an interest, one that was viewed by the masses as esoteric and possibly even frivolous.

During that period, numismatics came to be known as "the hobby of kings." Not until the 20th century would it gain such popularity among the American public that it could rightly be called "the king of hobbies."

▶ Coin Collecting in the United States

The United States Mint came into being in 1792 and issued its first coins for general circulation the following year. There were, however, few collectors to set those coins aside in the 13 original states and the first few that followed. Indeed, the preservation of pristine early examples is attributable largely to hobbyists in Europe, particularly England, who made it a point to acquire mint-fresh specimens of coinage from the likewise mint-fresh nation.

Coin collecting wouldn't gain a firm foothold in the United States for more than half a century. There were some home-grown collectors, to be sure, but they were extremely few. Most early Americans had little time to spare for diversions of this sort, for their waking hours were spent attaining the necessities of life for themselves and their families.

Among the few collectors in the nation's formative years was a young Philadelphian named Joseph Mickley. He developed an interest in coins after noticing how difficult it was to locate copper cents dated 1799—which happened to be his birth year. The difficulty was understandable, for the Mint's output of cents had been minuscule that year. Mickley soon became an enthusiastic collector of U.S. coinage in general, and he made it a practice to visit the

Mint—conveniently located right in his hometown—and acquire new coins as they were released. On one such expedition, in 1827, he purchased at face value four newly made quarter dollars. These turned out to be great rarities, and today each is valued at tens of thousands of dollars.

1799 large cent. Joseph Mickley's inability to find this scarce coin from his birth year led him to become one of the earliest U.S. coin collectors. *Photos courtesy Bowers & Merena Galleries.*

Coin collecting's base expanded considerably in the United States in the late 1850's, thanks in large measure to a highly visible change in the size and composition of the cent. Up to that time, the cent had been a pure copper coin almost as large and heavy as the present-day half dollar. With copper prices rising and many Americans grumbling about the "large cent's" inconvenient heft, Congress authorized a much smaller substitute—the same diameter as today's Lincoln cent but 50 percent heavier—made of a whitish-gray copper-nickel alloy.

The new cent proved highly popular, and the widespread publicity surrounding its release prompted many people to take a closer look at the now-obsolete copper cents, as well as the pure copper half cents, which also were removed from production at the time. Meaningful numbers of people went on to become collectors. Not coincidentally, 1858 saw the founding of the first national coin-hobby organization in the country—the New York City-based American Numismatic and Archaeological Society, which later shortened its name to simply the American Numismatic Society, or ANS.

❯ Out of the Depths of Depression

Coin collecting, American-style, enjoyed steady growth during the next 75 years. With the ANS emphasizing scholarly pursuits and concentrating heavily on the study and display of ancient coinage, rather than U.S. issues, hobbyists banded together in 1891 to form a new organization that would give greater weight to coins from their own country. They called it the American Numismatic Association, or ANA, and today it is considered to be the national coin club, with upwards of 25,000 members spread throughout the 50 states.

The next dramatic shot in the arm for U.S. coin collecting occurred in the early 1930's—ironically as a result of the Great Depression. Millions of Americans found themselves with unwanted time on their hands, and little money in their pockets, because of the economic ravages that decimated the work force during that dreary decade. They filled the time, without emptying their pockets, through a series of inexpensive pastimes: going to movies, playing miniature golf, solving crossword puzzles, piecing together jigsaw puzzles and filling "penny boards."

Penny boards were 11-by-14-inch heavy cardboard holders with die-cut holes in which all the U.S. coins of a given type and series could be displayed. The basic board was designed to hold Lincoln cents, but boards were available for other coins as well. The idea was to assemble a complete set of coins—one for each date from every mint—from pocket change, an investment that required just the modest face value of the coins. A Wisconsin entrepreneur named J. K. Post devised this clever novelty, and he had the boards produced by the Whitman Publishing Co. of Racine, Wis. Whitman officials were impressed with the boards' simplicity and wide public appeal, and in 1934 the company bought out Post. Thereafter, Whitman used its marketing clout to distribute the coin boards even more widely.

The penny boards drew many thousands of new collectors into the hobby, democratizing it and laying a solid foundation for the vastly greater expansion that would follow in the century's second half.

▶ The Fifties and Sixties

Coin collecting tapered off during World War II, as new priorities preoccupied Americans. They were back to work again—millions of them in uniform—and had less idle time for recreation. More important, their minds were focused on the larger issues of war, peace, survival, separation from loved ones and triumph over tyranny abroad. The hobby resumed its pattern of growth once victory was achieved, but a decade or more would pass before it gained enough new momentum to experience another major surge.

Two elements figured most strongly in that surge, and both began to command collectors' attention in 1950. One was the sale of *proof sets* by the U.S. Mint. The other was an appetite for *rolls* of newly issued U.S. coins and other late-date coins that were still in mint condition because they never had been released into circulation.

Proof sets (discussed more fully in Chapter 7) are annual sets containing specially struck, virtually flawless examples of current-year U.S. coins. The Mint had made such coins for sale to the general public off and on since 1858, but had suspended their production in 1942 because of wartime limitations. Interest was high when it lifted the suspension in 1950: The Mint sold 51,386 sets that year, more than double the previous high of 21,120 in 1942. Within a few years, however, that figure seemed puny. Sales nearly doubled annually in a six-year period starting in 1952—so that by 1957, they had soared to 1,247,952 sets. They would reach a peak of 3,950,762 sets in 1964 before the Mint halted their production once again—this time because of a nationwide coin shortage that forced it to concentrate on manufacturing coins for circulation.

The proof coins undeniably were lustrous and appealing. Their main attraction, however, was their price: From 1950 through 1964, the Mint sold the sets for just $2.10 apiece, and they traded for more than that in the resale market—sometimes substantially more—as soon as they hit the street. For that reason, many people, including noncollectors, purchased them in quantity from the Mint and then either sold them at a quick profit or set them aside for the long haul, perhaps as a nest egg for retirement or their children's education.

The 1950 event that triggered collectors' interest in rolls was the unusually low production of Jefferson nickels at the branch mint in Denver. Only 2,630,030 five-cent pieces were made that year at the Denver Mint—a figure that remains the lowest ever for any regular-issue date-and-mint combination in the Jefferson nickel series. Coin dealers soon began promoting this coin as an instant rarity and selling it in bank-wrapped rolls—with 40 coins to the roll—at steadily increasing multiples of face value. This, in turn, ignited a contagion that spread to rolls of other modern U.S. coins in mint condition, particularly Lincoln cents. Along with late-date proof sets, late-date rolls would dominate the market through the early 1960's and prices would rise to levels that in time proved unsupportable. The 1950-D Jefferson nickel remained in the forefront of this ever-rising curve, reaching the rarefied height of $1,200 per roll—or $30 per coin—before it came crashing

down along with all the other modern rolls. Today, it can be purchased for less than $10 per coin and actually is scarcer (although
not more valuable) in circulated shape than in mint condition,
because so much of its output was set aside and saved when it first
came out.

The mid-1960's proved disastrous for the hobby. The speculative bubble surrounding late-date coin rolls burst as the decade
neared its midpoint. Proof set production was halted, and Treasury
officials prevailed upon Congress to authorize the removal of silver
from the Roosevelt dime and Washington quarter starting in 1965
and reduce the silver content in the Kennedy half dollar from 90
percent to just 40 percent. (It, too, would become a totally silverless
coin in 1971.) Thus began the era of base-metal "clad" U.S.
coinage—coinage with little or no intrinsic value, inordinately
high mintage levels and generally inferior quality. To make matters
worse, Gresham's Law kicked in, and people began removing pre-
1965 half dollars, quarters and dimes from circulation, anticipat-
ing—correctly—that they would command a premium because of
their precious-metal content.

▶ The 50 State Quarters Program

From the mid-1960's to the late 1990's, major changes occurred in
the way U.S. coins were viewed by the people who acquired them.
The emphasis shifted away from the *hobby* or *collecting* aspects of
obtaining scarce coins to the *business* or *investing* side. In large part,
this was due to the far-ranging flight of collectors from the field.
This exodus began when the roll market collapsed and accelerated
when base-metal coinage flooded into commerce and silver
coinage quickly disappeared. All at once, there was little or no
incentive to seek out late-date rolls, and almost nothing collectible
left in circulation. Up to then, dimes, quarters and half dollars dat-

ing back decades had been readily available in pocket change. Now, there was almost nothing but the newly minted copper-nickel "sandwich-type" coins. Even cents and nickels—the two coins unaffected by the change in composition—underwent a purge whereby older coins were saved in massive numbers. In the case of the cent, people started setting aside all of the so-called "wheat-ears" coins struck from 1909 to 1958, which bore two sheafs of wheat on the reverse, leaving only the Lincoln Memorial cents—recently introduced in 1959—to serve the nation's needs. With nickels, the result was a very hasty exit for the popular Buffalo nickel, which up to then had managed to maintain a respectable presence. All too soon, the great old coin was gone and Jefferson nickels had the field to themselves.

Some pure collectors continued their pursuits, but far less conspicuously. With little incentive to search through rolls and bags for valuable coins, as multitudes had done up to 1965, many adherents abandoned the hobby and took up other forms of recreation. For the same reason, far fewer youngsters embraced coin collecting to begin with. Instead, they turned to comic books, baseball cards, video games and other more instantly gratifying ways to fill their idle hours

The thrill of discovery finally returned in 1999, when the U.S. Mint issued the first of the 50 State Quarters. After a generation in the wilderness, Americans had something worthwhile to look for again in everyday pocket change, and children had a truly compelling reason to begin collecting coins. Washington quarters with special designs honoring various states began to appear in circulation, giving people an incentive to sort through the coins in their pockets, purses and pay envelopes. In all, there were to be 50 special 25-cent pieces, issued at the rate of five coins per year for a full decade.

Millions joined the treasure hunt, purchasing folders, boards and maps to house and display their 50 State Quarters as they continued to track down the coins in circulation. They watched with keen interest to see when their own state's coin, and coins from neighboring states, would take their place in the lengthening parade. Once they became caught up in the excitement, many of them decided to explore U.S. coinage a bit more fully and see what other coins might pique their interest. In short, they became collectors.

The 50 State Quarters Program quickly proved to be the single greatest boost the hobby had received in most collectors' memory—possibly *ever*. With new statehood quarters scheduled to appear roughly every 10 weeks through 2008, the dividends seemed likely to continue and compound. The series will be examined in detail in Chapter 9.

....

Chapter 2

Ways to Collect

....

Coin collecting is every bit as diverse as coins themselves. Some approaches to the hobby enjoy greater popularity than others, to be sure—partly because books and periodicals focus more intensively on these areas, partly because albums and other supplies for housing and displaying coins are more readily available for these and partly because they are simply more appealing to a wider circle of collectors. The dedicated enthusiast is limited, however, only by his or her imagination. Budget constraints put certain coins beyond some people's reach, of course, but virtually anyone—on virtually any budget—can find a collecting niche that will be interesting, challenging and fulfilling.

Typically, most collectors begin by setting aside coins that they encounter in everyday use. That's why the 50 State Quarters Program has been such a powerful catalyst in energizing the hobby at the grass-roots level. After decades of bland sameness when U.S. coinage art remained depressingly static, Americans began to see intriguing new designs on the Washington quarter's reverse, not just once a decade or even once a year, but once every 10 weeks. They could find these coins in pocket change with just a little searching, and save one example of each for an outlay of only 25 cents apiece.

Lincoln cents also have been responsible for bringing many recruits into the fold—just as Indian Head cents and pure copper "large cents" had done in earlier times. Here, the initial "invest-ment" is just one cent when an eye-catching coin is found in cir-culation—an important consideration, at least in years gone by, for youngsters with only modest resources. Since the cent normally is made in substantially greater quantities than coins of higher denominations, and with correspondingly more minting mistakes and varieties, both of which are considered highly collectible, the chances of finding worthwhile coins are enhanced.

1991 British sovereign. This gold coin, issued with this reverse since 1817, has one of the world's most famous coin designs, showing St. George slaying the dragon. *Photos courtesy British Royal Mint.*

▶ Foreign and Ancient Coins

The world of coins encompasses coins from the entire world—and not only from today's world but from countries and societies cov-ering a period of more than 25 centuries. This gives collectors a broad spectrum from which to choose historically, geographically and culturally. Many do pursue foreign and ancient coins, as they are described in numismatic shorthand, but most American hobby-ists concentrate on coins from their own country. Some may dis-miss this as heedless chauvinism—even xenophobia. In truth, it simply reflects the fact that when the hobby spread from the draw-ing room to the living room in homes across the United States during the middle years of the 20th century, it did so almost exclu-sively in ways that featured U.S. coins. Then, when the hobby continued its expansion and a broader marketplace sprang up to serve it, U.S. coinage continued to be the focus.

1999 five-pound British memorial coin for Diana, Princess of Wales. A numismatic tribute embraced by collectors around the world. *Photos courtesy British Royal Mint.*

2002 five-pound British golden jubilee crown of Queen Elizabeth II. A numismatic tribute for the Queen's 50th anniversary on the throne. *Photos courtesy British Royal Mint.*

Any coins issued by countries other than the United States are, of course, *foreign* in relation to U.S. coinage. Collectors tend to use this term primarily, however, to describe modern coins, especially contemporary issues, from other countries. The *Standard Catalog of World Coins*, a book the size of a large-city telephone directory, is considered the primary reference work on foreign coins, and it confines its coverage to the period from 1601 to the present. Coins of antiquity, especially Greek and Roman, are said to be *ancient*, while specialists also recognize such categories as Byzantine, Islamic and Oriental coins. Canadian and Mexican coins, coming from next-door neighbors, are collected more widely than most "foreign" issues, and occupy a special niche almost as extensions of U.S. coinage—numismatic "free trade zone" partners, so to speak.

1958 Canadian silver dollar. This coin's unusual totem pole design makes it a favorite with American collectors. *Photos courtesy Krause Publications.*

▶ Paper Money

Most people think of paper money as something to spend, not save, and certainly not as something to collect. Like coins, however, paper money comes under the umbrella definition of *numismatics*— the study and systematic acquisition of various forms of money as collectibles.

There are obvious drawbacks to collecting paper money. For one thing, it's less durable than coinage and more prone to serious damage with only minor mishandling. For another, its face value tends to be much higher than that of most coins, so setting it aside requires a greater outlay—even when it's obtained without paying a premium. A word of caution is in order: Although this is known as "folding money," it's not a good idea to fold paper money that may be worth a premium as a collectible. Hobbyists prefer bills that are "crisp uncirculated," and when a crisp new bill is folded in half for the very first time, its potential value in collectors' eyes is also halved—possibly even quartered.

Paper money's origin is less well defined than that of coins. A form of paper money bearing the seal of the emperor is known to have been in use in China, however, at the time Marco Polo visited that land in the late 13th century. Lack of public confidence inhib ited general use of paper currency down through the centuries— for whereas gold and silver coins possess intrinsic worth that reinforces their stated value as money, paper is utterly worthless and money made of paper derives its value exclusively from the trust its users have in the issuing government.

Paper money in the form of *Continental currency* was issued to help finance the American Revolution, but it ended up having little or no redemption value, giving rise to the expression "as worthless as a Continental." The federal government didn't issue paper money during the nation's early years, but many banks issued notes that served as money substitutes, at least until the banks went out of business—whereupon the now worthless bills became known as *broken bank notes.*

The outbreak of the Civil War in 1861 led to the authorization of the first federal paper money and the establishment of the U.S. Bureau of Engraving and Printing (BEP) to produce it. Necessity was the mother of this invention: The Union needed large sums of money to finance its war effort and, to a lesser extent, alternative forms of money were needed to replace the nation's coinage supply, which was quickly hoarded soon after hostilities commenced.

Just as the first U.S. cents were much heftier than the modern-day version, the first U.S. paper money was considerably bigger than the kind in use today. The parallel carries over to the names by which collectors know them—*large cents* and *large-size notes*. Early paper money also came to be known by a colorful nickname: People called them *horse blankets* in a tongue-in-cheek reference to their size. Skilled engravers at the BEP made good use of the bills' large surfaces by creating a profusion of exquisite and intricate designs featuring such themes as the landing of Columbus, the baptism of Pocahontas, the Battle of Lexington and the signing of the Declaration of Independence.

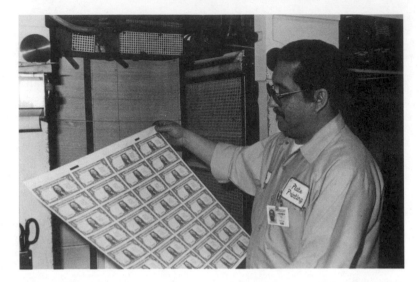

A workman examining a 32-note sheet of $1 bills at the U.S. Bureau of Engraving and Printing.

By the 1920's, the BEP's production had increased exponentially over earlier levels and the government was purchasing much larger quantities of the special highgrade paper that it used to print the currency. To cut down on this cost and also with an eye to public convenience, the Treasury trimmed its notes in 1929 to the much more modest size they have been ever since. While certainly cheaper and probably more convenient, this led to a set of designs that was sterile artistically. From that point onward, U.S. paper money became bland and predictable, with portraits of famous Americans, most of them U.S. presidents, on the face and depictions of well-known buildings or simply ornate inscriptions on the back. At one time, small-size notes were issued for public use in denominations as high as $10,000, but after World War II the BEP halted production of all bills above $100. In addition to the $10,000 bill, denominations of $500, $1,000 and $5,000 were issued. Most existing bills in those face values have been retired, but some survive in collections and command modest premiums, even in used condition, when they change hands.

▶ Dates and Mint Marks

Foreign and ancient coins have their devotees, and paper money boasts its share of enthusiasts, but mainstream numismatists in the United States concentrate overwhelmingly on U.S. coinage. Lincoln cents and 50-state Washington quarters have played the principal roles in attracting new collectors in recent years, but once recruits join the ranks, they branch out in many directions. Silver dollars—especially the Morgan type (named for its designer, George T. Morgan)—perennially rank among the most popular series. Buffalo nickels and Indian Head cents enjoy tremendous affection, and that puts them high on many collectors' lists of favorites. More advanced (and more affluent) hobbyists often find gold coins appealing.

No matter which series they gravitate toward, new collectors soon become aware that a very small feature found on many coins can have a big impact on their rarity and value. This is the letter or letters known as a *mint mark*, and its presence—or absence—denotes the minting facility where the coin was made.

For nearly half a century in the very early days of U.S. coinage, there was no reason for a mint mark, since all of the coins were made at the Philadelphia Mint, the only U.S. mint in existence at the time. As the nation grew, Congress saw a need to establish branch mints to facilitate coin production and distribution. In the late 1830's, it authorized three such mints—in New Orleans, whose central location gave it ready access to newly assimilated states along the Mississippi River; and in Charlotte, N.C., and Dahlonega, Ga., two cities in the heart of a major gold-mining region in the Southeast, whose raw material they could readily transform into coinage. To distinguish their coins from those made elsewhere, these mints stamped each coin with a letter denoting its place of origin—"O" for New Orleans, "C" for Charlotte and "D" for Dahlonega. With the discovery of gold in California and silver at the Comstock Lode in Nevada, branch mints were established in San Francisco in 1854 and Carson City in 1870 and their coins carried mint marks of "S" and "CC," respectively.

The Southern mints fell under Confederate control during the Civil War and two of them—Charlotte and Dahlonega—never reopened. The New Orleans Mint was reactivated in 1879, but its doors were closed for good in 1909. By then, a new branch, launched in 1906, was operating in Denver and using a "D" mint mark. The Philadelphia, Denver and San Francisco mints remain in operation today, along with a small branch mint at West Point, N.Y., on the grounds of the U.S. Military Academy, that joined them in 1984. Until recent years, virtually all coins from Philadelphia were identified by the *absence* of a mint mark; since the late 1970's, though, the mother mint has placed a "P" on all its coins except cents. The West Point Mint uses a "W" mint mark.

▶ 'Key' and Common-Date Coins

Mint marks' importance stems from the fact that production of a given coin during a certain year can vary widely from mint to mint—and while it may be abundant elsewhere, it may be extremely low at one particular facility. Through the years, output has generally been lower at branch mints because they are smaller than the main mint in Philadelphia, with more limited production capacity. In 1909, for instance, the Philadelphia Mint struck ample quantities of the then brand-new Lincoln cent, but production was very small in San Francisco. As a result, 1909-S Lincoln cents command substantial premiums, while 1909 cents without a mint mark (made in Philadelphia) have only nominal value as collectibles. On

Lincoln cents, the mint mark can be found directly below the date. Its location varies on other coins, but it is placed most frequently either under the date or at the base of the coin's reverse.

Coins with the lowest mintages are said to be the *key coins* in a series, and those that are somewhat more available but nonetheless scarce are called *semi-key coins*. These are the coins that hold the key to forming a complete collection of the series—a set that includes examples from every year and from every mint that struck the coin that year. Coins that are readily available are described as *common-date* issues.

"Date-and-mint" collecting is one of the most basic—and most popular—methods of approaching the hobby. Using this approach, collectors of Lincoln cents, for example, seek to acquire not only one cent from every year since the series' inception in 1909, but one cent from each mint for every date as well. Since the low-mintage cents of 1931 were made in small numbers at three different mints, a complete date-and-mint set would have to contain cents from all three mints—Philadelphia, Denver and San Francisco. Albums and folders produced to house U.S. coins encourage and facilitate this approach by providing holes for each date and mint-mark variety in a series.

▶ The Rise of 'Type' Collecting

Date-and-mint collecting was easier—and cheaper—in bygone days, when many of the coins in certain U.S. series could be found without great difficulty in ordinary pocket change or, if necessary, purchased from dealers for relatively modest premiums. As recently as the early 1950's, coins dating back to the late 19th century turned up with some frequency in everyday circulation. The exodus of older coins accelerated soon thereafter—first when the Lincoln cent was partially redesigned in 1959 to show the Lincoln Memorial on its reverse and then when the silver content was removed from the dime and quarter, and reduced in the half dollar, in 1965. In both cases, coins predating the changes were systematically pulled out of circulation, and before long almost all had vanished from the channels of commerce.

At that point, it became necessary to purchase almost *all* the coins needed for a date-and-mint collection. Moreover, the premiums had risen considerably as the growing number of hobbyists caused ever greater demand for the static—even shrinking—supply of coins. In the 1970's, as quality-conscious investors began to buy coins with a view to future profit, strong new emphasis was placed on coins' level of preservation—in other words, their grade.

Taking all these factors into account, many collectors decided to assemble sets of coins by *type,* rather than date and mint. Instead of acquiring one example for every date and every mint, they settled for just one coin—without regard to date and mint—to represent an entire series. A 20th-century type set, for instance, would contain one coin from every different series issued by the Mint during the 1900's—one Lincoln cent, one Buffalo nickel, one Washington quarter and so on. Since the date and mint didn't really matter, many chose to acquire common-date pieces—but to buy them in the highest grade levels they could afford. This greatly enhanced the appearance of their sets without requiring inordinate outlays. In fact, the total cost of such a type set more than likely would be less than the cost of a date-and-mint set in only average condition for most single 20th-century series.

❱ One Man's Complete Collection

Completeness is a virtue with coin collections; in a real sense, a complete collection is more than just the sum of its parts, for it underscores the dedication and effort that went into assembling it

Louis E. Eliasberg Sr. with a chart showing the growth of his Baltimore finance company. His coin collection also grew nicely, eventually selling for $44 million. *Photo courtesy American Numismatic Association.*

piece by piece. This can translate into substantial added value in the case of well-known collections.

The ultimate collection was the one formed between 1925 and 1950 by Louis E. Eliasberg Sr., a Baltimore financier who loaned money to others and bought money himself in the form of rare and valuable U.S. coins. During that quarter century, a time when the coin market hadn't yet fully emerged from its cocoon and prices were laughably low by current standards, Eliasberg parlayed substantial resources, business acumen and a fair share of good fortune into the acquisition of a complete date-and-mint collection of federal U.S. coinage—the only such collection ever known to exist. He filled the final hole in 1950 when he purchased the 1873-CC "no-arrows" dime (a dime produced at the Carson City Mint in 1873 without arrows beside the date). Mint records indicate that

12,400 examples of this coin were produced, but hobbyists now believe that the specimen acquired by Eliasberg is unique.

Eliasberg's feat was heralded by the media, including an extensive word-and-picture story in *Life* magazine which gave tremendous exposure to coin collecting and awakened many Americans to the hobby's possibilities. Eliasberg provided positive reinforcement by exhibiting his collection on a number of occasions over the years. In 1982, six years after his death, his heirs sold the gold portion of the collection at a glittering New York auction conducted by Bowers and Ruddy. The coins realized more than $11 million, even though the market was in a depression at the time. A decade and a half later, in 1996 and 1997, the rest of the collection was sold by the company's successor firm, Bowers and Merena—and this time the bottom line was $32.4 million. The overall total of $44 million is the most ever paid for any single coin collection sold at public auction, and there isn't any question that its fame—which rested on its completeness—helped push the figure higher than it would have been without that prestigious pedigree.

Chapter 3

··

The Coin Market

··

"Coin dealer" is a job description all but unheard of until modern times. Merchants bought and sold rare and desirable coins in bygone days, to be sure, but almost always simply as an adjunct to some other commercial pursuit—a jewelry business, perhaps, or a pawn shop. In olden days, when coin collecting was limited to just a privileged few, merchants who came into possession of such coins might take them for inspection by a nobleman or ecclesiastic known to have an interest. More often than not, the "coin dealers" of those dimly remembered days were money changers by trade.

The few coin collectors in the young United States of the early and mid-1800's were concentrated in cities along the Eastern Seaboard—notably Philadelphia, Boston and New York—and that's where the earliest coin dealers set up shop in the second half of the century, though certainly nothing remotely resembling the typical coin shop of today. One of the major coin dealerships of the modern era, Stack's of New York, traces its roots to the late 1850's—but at that time, it handled coins only as part of a foreign-exchange business in lower Manhattan. It would not evolve into a primarily numismatic enterprise until the 1930's.

The first professional numismatist (a fancy name for coin dealer) in the United States is believed to have been Edward

Cogan, who began dealing in coins in 1858 in Philadelphia. Cogan had sailed to America five years earlier, at the age of 50, from his native England and had opened a store where he dealt in curios and art objects. His expansion into numismatic items coincided with the burgeoning interest in coins spawned by the introduction of the small-size U.S. cent in 1857. In November 1858, Cogan conducted a mail-bid sale of coins—perhaps America's first—in which he offered 77 lots through a two-page leaflet. The 19 successful bidders acquired these treasures for a total of $128.63. Cogan moved his business to Brooklyn in 1865, because he saw New York as a market with greater potential.

Looking back, it seems appropriate that a transplanted Briton should have been the one to usher in the U.S. coin marketplace, since British collectors had played a pivotal role in preserving choice examples of early U.S. coinage and thereby planting the seeds for the hobby's eventual growth in the United States. Philadelphian Joseph Mickley and other home-grown hobbyists—among them Matthew Stickney of Salem, Mass., and Jeremiah Colburn of Boston—formed important collections in the early 1800's, including many U.S. coins found in circulation, obtained from banks or purchased at face value from the Mint. However, without the keen interest of hobbyists abroad, and especially in England, pristine examples of the earliest U.S. coins might have all entered the channels of commerce, and thus been lost in that level of preservation to future generations of collectors.

The coin business, like the coin hobby, experienced steady growth from 1858 onward. Cogan was soon joined by another important dealer, W. Elliott Woodward of Roxbury, Mass., near Boston—and Woodward began to conduct ever bigger auction sales. One such sale, cataloged by Woodward in 1864, consisted of more than 3,000 lots and realized the then-record sum of slightly more than $13,000. The Civil War delayed the full flowering of

American numismatics, but it picked up added steam after hostilities ended in 1865. In May 1866, just 13 months after the war's conclusion, the American Numismatic and Archaeological Society published the first issue of the *American Journal of Numismatics,* which quickly established itself as the leading periodical in the field. This was another important step forward in laying a firm foundation for the coin collecting hobby in this country—and, by extension, the market that would serve coin hobbyists' needs.

▶ As the Century Turned

By the end of the nineteenth century, collectors had access to a small but thriving network of coin dealers, primarily along the Eastern Seaboard. Leading dealers included the Chapman brothers of Philadelphia and Edward Frossard, Lyman H. Low and the Scott Stamp and Coin Company of New York. A 1900 survey found that there were 21 full-time and part-time coin dealers in the country and several thousand collectors. The American Numismatic Association, not yet 10 years old, had more than 300 members.

U.S. coinage itself was less than inspiring—and distinctly old-fashioned—in appearance. All four gold coins then being issued bore designs dating back to the first half of the 1800's—some of them all the way back to the late 1830's. That would soon change: During the decade-and-a-half from 1907 through 1921, the coinage would undergo a complete artistic makeover that would elevate it to an aesthetic peak never achieved before—and, sad to say, never approached since—in the nation's history.

Coin prices advanced considerably between the late 1850's and the early 1900's, but remained ludicrously low by latter-day standards. In 1907, a Brasher doubloon—an extremely rare Colonial gold coin struck privately in 1787 by New York City jeweler

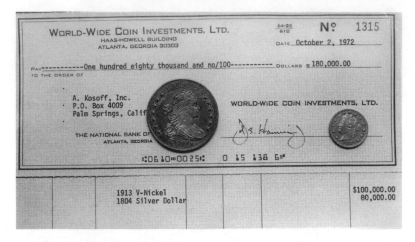

A check marking the sale of two great numismatic rarities in 1972. At the time, both prices were records. Today, the two coins would cost well over a million dollars apiece.

Ephraim Brasher—changed hands at a Chapman auction for $6,200 and promptly was proclaimed "the world's highest priced coin." The next time the same coin appeared on the auction block, in November 1979, it reclaimed that title—but this time the selling price was $725,000. At the same 1907 auction, an 1804 silver dollar brought $3,600—a record at the time for this great U.S. rarity. Since 1997, several 1804 dollars have realized prices in excess of a million dollars at public auctions, including one that fetched the unprecedented sum of more than $4 million at a New York City sale in August 1999. That was well over twice the previous auction record for any single coin.

The reasonable prices of rare coins in the late 1800's and early 1900's enabled numismatists of that era to assemble impressive collections for relatively modest outlays. One prominent turn-of-the-century hobbyist, wealthy Chicago brewer Virgil Brand, outdid all of his contemporaries in his relentless drive to capitalize on this advantageous market situation. Between the mid-1880's, when he started collecting coins, and his death at age 60 in 1926, Brand acquired some 325,000 coins—many of them major rarities which would bring tens of thousands of dollars, even hundreds of thousands of dollars, if offered for sale today. He carefully placed these coins in small, fully annotated brown kraft envelopes that he then stored in hundreds of cigar boxes in his Chicago apartment. Brand is recalled not only for the vastness of his numismatic holdings, undoubtedly the most extensive collection of truly rare coins ever formed, but also for the highly eccentric behavior that led to his demise. He died of food poisoning that he contracted after eating in an unsanitary restaurant that catered primarily to the indigent.

As the ranks of collectors swelled in the early 1900's, important new dealers entered the market to serve their needs. Among them were Thomas L. Elder, Wayte Raymond and the Guttag Brothers, all of New York City, and Burdette G. Johnson of St. Louis. One dealer towers above the rest for the role he played in popularizing the hobby and attracting untold numbers of new collectors. B. Max Mehl was his name, and publicity was his game. During a career spanning more than half a century, from his first fixed price list in 1904 to his death in 1957, Mehl advertised constantly—and cleverly—in Sunday newspaper supplements, on the radio and even on matchbook covers, touting the hobby and, of course, his company, which was based in Fort Worth, Tex. His catchy, effective advertisements earned him recognition as "the P. T. Barnum of numismatics."

One of Mehl's primary pitches was an offer to pay $50—a sizable sum at the time—for any 1913 Liberty Head nickel. He never had to make good on the offer, and never expected to, since—as he was well aware—only five examples of this coin were (and are) known to exist. (The coin is described in detail in a later chapter.) The offer, however, intrigued the countless non-collectors who

Texas coin dealer B. Max Mehl. The man who made the 1913 Liberty nickel famous. *Photo courtesy American Numismatic Association.*

saw or heard it, and many of them sent a dollar to Mehl for his *Star Rare Coin Encyclopedia,* a booklet that also was part of the pitch. He made a handsome profit from these orders and, more important, drew a small army of newcomers into the hobby.

▶ How a Hobby Became a Big Business

The coin market's growth accelerated sharply in the 1950's and 1960's. Americans had increasing amounts of discretionary income available, plus more free time to enjoy it—and many were devoting part of that money and time to the acquisition of coins, particularly proof sets and rolls of modern issues. New coin shops opened across the country, existing ones expanded and mail-order business picked up dramatically. New hobby periodicals began publication and helped establish links between buyers and sellers. *Numismatic News* was first, in 1952, followed by *Coin World, Coins Magazine* and *COINage* in the early 1960's. *Coin World*'s debut, in April 1960, was especially significant, for it was the first numismatic periodical to appear on a weekly basis, underscoring the scope of the hobby's explosive development. Along with the *Numismatic Scrapbook Magazine,* which had been around since 1935, the ever-thicker issues of these new publications offered evidence of a marketplace blossoming before their readers' eyes.

By 1962, the coin market had shed its somewhat sedate image and exuded a brand of brash hucksterism even B. Max Mehl might have found a bit excessive. Trouble lay ahead, however, for the boom in proof sets and rolls was based more on speculative fever than on solid collecting principles—and by 1965, both dealers and collectors with shallow hobby roots were taking flight.

The coin market drifted for a few years thereafter. Buying up stashes of silver U.S. coins for eventual melting provided a diversion for dealers who had persevered following the crash. So did the purchase of silver certificates—blue-seal U.S. paper money that remained redeemable in silver until June 24, 1968 and therefore worth a premium over face value. The U.S. Mint resumed production of proof sets in 1968 after a three-year hiatus, and that helped stimulate interest as well. Yet another catalyst came along in 1972, when the General Services Administration, a U.S. government agency, held the first in a series of mail-bid sales to disperse a hoard of scarce old silver dollars found in federal vaults a decade earlier. The coins had come to light in the early 1960's when savvy Americans descended upon the Treasury in Washington with satchels full of silver certificates and exchanged the paper money for silver dollars. After thousands of bags of mostly common "cartwheels" had been dispersed, bags of low-mintage coins—primarily from the Carson City Mint—were discovered at the bottom of the long-dormant piles, where they had lain concealed for nearly a century. Recognizing the value of these coins, the Treasury had set them aside and halted redemption of silver certificates with dollar coins, redeeming them instead with grains of silver.

◗ Collecting and Investing

In the early 1970's, a new kind of coin dealer emerged. Instead of doing business in a shop with a casual atmosphere, this new breed tended to operate out of a suite of offices—wearing a three-piece suit instead of informal attire. Coins now went into *portfolios,* rather than collections. And the emphasis was on *investment potential,* rather than collectibility. Following the collapse of the market in late-date proof sets and rolls, the pendulum already had swung toward older, scarcer coins in superior condition, sold individually rather than by the roll. With the advent of the investment marketplace, this swing became more pronounced. Marketing also underwent a drastic change: Instead of reaching out to traditional collectors through advertisements in hobby periodicals, many of the new dealers targeted doctors, dentists, lawyers and other professionals by placing ads in magazines serving those fields. Numismatic knowledge was not a prerequisite for responding; in fact, the less that prospective clients knew about rare coins, the better—at least in the view of some such dealers.

From that time onward, the coin market has functioned for all intents and purposes on two tiers—one for collectors and the other for investors. There is overlap between them, to be sure: Whether they admit it or not, many collectors keep track of their coins' price performance and potential; and some coin buyers who enter the field as investors begin to take an interest in the stories behind their coins and find themselves transformed into collector/ investors. The fundamental difference lies in the two groups' motivation in acquiring coins: Collectors do it mainly for pleasure, investors primarily for profit.

From the outset, noncollectors purchasing coins as investments showed a decided preference for lustrous, pristine specimens free from wear and flaws. That had an immediate—and profound— effect on the prices of such material. Up to that time, values had tended to rise in a straight-line progression from the lowest-condition example of a given coin to the highest, with an uncirculated piece—one that never saw use in daily commerce   bringing perhaps 10 percent more than the next-highest grade of "about uncirculated," or AU, which applied to coins that had entered circulation but barely so. Since then, uncirculated coins often have been worth 10 *times* more—even 100 times more.

Many longtime collectors yearn for the preinvestment days when prices were low, good material was abundant and completing fine collections was a realistic goal even for budget-conscious hobbyists. Regrettably, those days are unlikely to return. On the other hand, it can be argued that the influx of investors—and investment-related money—reinvigorated the field at a time when market activity was at a historically low ebb. A case can also be made that the subsequent surge in value of "investment-grade" material put into proper perspective the true rarity, and thus the true value, of previously underpriced and underappreciated coins. In any event, collectors with limited resources still have the realm of circulated coinage pretty much to themselves, since most investors continue to shun anything less than the best—which in this case means uncirculated coins. And unlike their mint-condition cousins, circulated U.S. coins—including very scarce issues—have appreciated in value just moderately, on the whole, since the early 1970's.

▶ Ways to Buy and Sell Coins

Newcomers to the hobby, including the tens of millions introduced to coins by the 50-state Washington quarters, usually start out by looking for interesting pieces in pocket change. Their next step, as a rule, is to visit a local coin shop—perhaps to purchase a board or album to house and display their statehood quarters. This, then, becomes their baptism in buying coins or coin-related merchandise. While in the coin shop, many find their interest piqued by other inexpensive items—proof sets, for example, or coins no longer found in circulation, such as Buffalo nickels or Indian Head cents. Once they start to purchase other such material, they're well on their way to becoming full-fledged collectors.

The coin market offers a number of different avenues for buying and selling coins. Here are some of the routes most widely traveled:

▶ **Coin shops.** These provide an excellent starting point for buying coins—and eventually for selling them as well. Coin shops vary widely in size and sophistication; larger shops in major cities such as New York or Chicago are likely to carry a far more diverse and extensive inventory than mom-and-pop dealerships in small or midsize towns. On the other hand, smaller shops may be able to charge a smaller markup because they have lower operating costs than their big-city counterparts. New collectors buying less expensive coins can be reasonably confident they won't be "ripped off" in a coin shop because the dealers who operate such establishments have an ongoing presence in the community and can't afford to be tarred by bad publicity or negative word-of-mouth. Selling coins—a collection inherited from a relative, for example—is another matter. In such cases, the uninitiated should first read up on the subject; one excellent book is *The Coin Collector's Survival Manual* by Scott A. Travers (Bonus Books Inc., Chicago). They also should consult the Better Business Bureau to see if complaints have been lodged against any coin dealers in their area. Then they should seek estimates from several different dealers before deciding where to sell the coins. If they are selling a fairly large collection of more than just nominal value, they also might consider consigning the coins for sale at a public auction.

▶ ***Mail-order dealers.*** These provide a useful service for buyers who live in outlying areas, where there may not be a coin shop within easy driving distance. These dealers advertise regularly in hobby periodicals such as *Coin World, Numismatic News, COINage* and *Coins Magazine*. Mail-order dealers often specialize in certain coins—Lincoln cents, for instance—and have a wider selection of these coins than smaller shops. On the downside, buyers can't see coins before purchasing them, and this can result in frustration and disappointment—not to mention the inherent delay and added expense of buying coins by mail.

▶ ***Auction dealers.*** These dealers conduct public sales several times a year in major cities, and some also conduct mail-bid sales. The public sales, in particular, often are lavish events featuring hundreds—even thousands—of coins, many of them rare and valuable. Registered bidders signify their interest in a particular lot by raising numbered paddles and continue doing so until that lot is hammered down with the familiar cry of "Going, going, gone!" Typically, a buyer's fee—15 percent, as a rule—is added to the "hammer price" to help defray the dealer's costs. A catalog is published prior to the sale and distributed to prospective buyers, and many times such catalogs become collector's

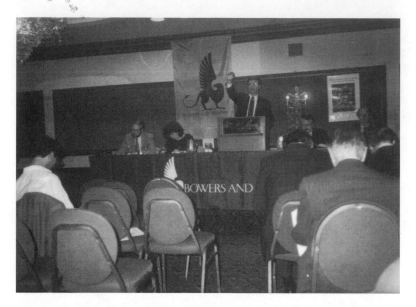

A major New York auction conducted by Bowers & Merena. William D. Hawfield, Jr., podium, is calling the sale. *Photo courtesy Scott A. Travers.*

items in their own right. This is a more advanced forum for buying coins, and newer collectors would be well advised to attend some public auctions as an observer before attempting to participate.

▶ *Coin shows.* Attending a coin show is one of the best ways to get a sense of the coin market's size and diversity. This is particularly true of major shows, such as the twice-yearly conventions of the American Numismatic Association, the three-times-a-year Long Beach (Calif.) Coin and Stamp Expo and the Florida United Numismatists (FUN) show, which draws thousands to the Sunshine State early each January to buy and sell coins and escape the snow and cold back home. A coin show invariably has a *bourse,* or sales area, where dealers offer coins and related items at long rows of booths. These bourses range from perhaps a dozen tables at small local shows to hundreds of booths at major events. At larger shows, there is literally something for everyone—a broad selection of coins from every U.S. series, plus foreign and ancient coins, paper money, medals, tokens and books. With so much competition just around every corner, bourse dealers frequently will bargain with would-be buyers. Even for those "just looking," this is a marvelous opportunity to see a wealth of material at a single time and place.

....

Chapter 4

Supply and Demand

....

Collectors may downplay the cost of the coins they buy, and their investment potential, but value is a subject of considerable interest to many outsiders. More often than not, the yardsticks they apply are wildly inaccurate—even totally irrelevant—and they become incredulous when told that perfectly normal-looking coins are worth exponentially more than the odd ones they may have in their possession.

They're amazed, for instance, to learn that many coins minted in ancient Rome are worth just a few dollars, while some coins produced by the United States Mint within the last decade have changed hands for tens of thousands of dollars. That's because *age* is not a key determinant of numismatic value.

Neither is *beauty*. Aesthetic appeal is surely a plus; everything else being equal, most collectors would rather have a coin with a beautiful design than one that is plain-looking or downright ugly. But beauty alone enhances a coin's value by only a nominal amount—if at all.

◗ The Elements of Value

With coins, as with most tangible objects, value is a function of *supply* and *demand*. It's determined by how many examples of a given coin are available, and how many people want such a coin.

Precious-metal content plays a part, of course, in establishing the value of a silver, gold or platinum coin—but only in setting a floor price. A coin that contains an ounce of precious metal is worth at least as much as the current market value of that metal. It may or may not have premium value—added value beyond its intrinsic worth—as a collectible.

Rarity

Rarity is an obvious component of this equation. People use the term "rare coins" to describe any coins that are collectible. Truly *rare* coins are, as the word suggests, not simply collectible but exceptionally scarce—available in very small numbers. Normally, this is because they were minted in small numbers to begin with. In some cases, however, it results from the fact that the coins' original mintages were dramatically reduced by subsequent events. That's what happened with certain U.S. gold coins produced in the late 1920's and early 1930's. Millions of these—in some cases almost the entire mintages—were stored in government vaults in 1933, when President Franklin D. Roosevelt issued his Gold Surrender Order. They were thereupon melted and converted into bars, along with the other gold coins turned in to the government by the public,

1894-S Barber dime. One of the greatest U.S. coin rarities, with an original mintage of just 24 examples. *Photo courtesy American Numismatic Association.*

leaving hardly any for collectors. Similarly, untold millions of U.S. silver coins were melted in 1979 and 1980, when the price of silver bullion soared, peaking at more than $50 an ounce in January 1980. Coins that had been quite common before the mass meltings are far more elusive today—not rare, perhaps, but certainly harder to find.

Quality

Quality plays a major role, as well, in determining the value of a coin. It stands to reason that a well-preserved example will bring a higher price than one that is worn, damaged or otherwise diminished in its aesthetic appeal. That was true even a hundred years ago, when coin prices moved at a far more leisurely pace and "condition" was not a crucial and constant concern for most collectors. Coins may have been bought and sold only in a few broad categories, essentially "new" and "used," but new ones still cost somewhat more than the rest. In recent years, since the advent of the investment-coin market, quality has become an all-consuming issue and this has been reflected in the price structure of most U.S. coins. Those in mint condition bring substantially higher prices than their circulated counterparts—even those with relatively little wear. And coins in *exceptional* mint condition often bring a great deal more than those in just *average* mint condition.

1916-D "Mercury" dime. A modern rarity and, in this case, a condition rarity as well, worth many thousands of dollars in this high level of preservation. *Photo courtesy Scott A. Travers/Bowers & Merena Galleries.*

Demand

At first, these spikes in the premium value of "mint-state" coins were primarily a function of *demand*. Investors, in particular, not only *prefer* high quality but *insist* upon it—and as the demand increased for the fixed supply of these coins, their prices rose. Then, as more and more coins were submitted to grading services (see Chapter 5), it became apparent that certain coins—though not especially scarce, and perhaps even plentiful, in lower mint-state grades—were exceedingly hard to find in the very highest grades. These became known as *condition rarities*—coins whose rarity stemmed directly and perhaps even exclusively from their condition. Production quality might have been poor that year at the mint where they were struck. Collectors might not have saved very many at the time, so almost all escaped into circulation. Whatever the reason or reasons, they were (and are) all but unattainable in the highest grades. Intense demand developed for these coins, acting now upon a much smaller supply. This combination soon drove their prices to new and spectacular heights.

▶ Modern Condition Rarities

Initially, the quest for condition-rarity coins centered around obsolete denominations and series—coins no longer seen in circulation. These included series from the start of U.S. coinage in 1793 through the early 1900's, particularly such widely collected coins as Morgan silver dollars and Saint-Gaudens double eagles ($20 gold pieces designed by famed sculptor Augustus Saint-Gaudens). In time, these became prohibitively expensive for many buyers, reducing the pool of potential customers, and some dealers sought to fill the market void by promoting pristine examples of modern—even current—U.S. coins, such as Lincoln cents and Jefferson nickels. These coins exist in vastly greater quantities than earlier series, but as with older series, they include some hard-to-find condition rarities—very high-grade coins that are genuinely scarce in that condition, even though they are properly dismissed as common-date coins overall.

Buying condition rarities requires care and knowledge, even when the purchase involves more seasoned series. Some Morgan dollars, for instance, are readily available in top mint condition and therefore aren't worth significantly more than lesser mint-state coins. There's simply too great a supply. The 1881 and 1882 silver dollars from the San Francisco Mint both fit this profile: Both are well-struck and lustrous as a rule, and both saw little use in circulation, so large numbers remain in top mint-state condition, having reposed in vaults and collections since the day they left the mint.

Even greater caution is called for when buying modern "condition rarities"—late-date coins that are touted as scarce and valuable primarily on the basis of extraordinary condition. Whereas older U.S. coins such as Morgan dollars often have mintages of only a few million for a given date and mint, modern coins were produced by the tens and hundreds of millions—even by the billions, in some instances. Thus, there's a substantial risk that rolls or even bags of these coins may emerge some day with hitherto unreported high-grade specimens, flooding the market with coins that were thought to be condition rarities and causing their prices to plunge. That is far less likely with the older series, not only because they have much lower mintages but also because their track records in the marketplace are much more solid and settled.

▶ The Demand Side

There are numbers on both sides of the supply-and-demand equation. Coins with very low mintage figures, or very small populations in top mint condition, are likely to command significant premiums based on rarity—a component of *supply*. Their value is also affected by the degree of *demand* that exists for them, and this can skew comparative values dramatically, making it crystal clear that rarity is relative.

Popularity enters the picture at this point. Some U.S. coins and series of coins are enormously popular, while others appeal to a much more limited audience. Lincoln cents and Morgan dollars are avidly pursued by legions of collectors, for example, while esoteric coins such as patterns—experimental pieces made to showcase new designs or metallic compositions, chiefly in the late 19th century—are collected by a relative handful of enthusiasts. The greater popularity of the cents and silver dollars translates into far more broad-based marketplace demand—and that, in turn, propels their premium value. Meanwhile, pattern coins may bring only modest premiums, and grow in value just gradually, even though they're far rarer in absolute terms.

1879 "Schoolgirl" pattern silver dollar. Although very rare, patterns such as this have a limited collector base, and that holds down their value. *Photo courtesy Scott A. Travers/Bowers & Merena Galleries.*

The upshot is that a Lincoln cent or Morgan dollar may be deemed "rare" with a mintage of 100,000—or even a million or more—and may command a higher price than a pattern coin of which fewer than 100 examples are known. For purposes of illustration, Exhibit A might be the 1914-D Lincoln cent, a coin produced at the branch mint in Denver that year. Its mintage is nearly 1.2 million, yet it sells for more than $100 even in well-worn condition, several thousand dollars in average mint condition—and a five-figure price in top mint condition. Mint-state examples of many U.S. pattern coins with mintages under 100 are worth substantially less than comparable examples of the 1914-D cent—even though they're more than a thousand times rarer.

1999 Susan B. Anthony dollar. In a popularity contest, this short-lived series would probably finish dead last. *Photo courtesy United States Mint.*

The key, of course, is that millions of collectors are putting together sets of Lincoln cents—and all of them covet the 1.2 million 1914-D cents, while there may not be even 100 specialists vying for the 100 examples of the much rarer pattern coin. Demand pushes coin prices higher only when it exceeds the available supply. Supply and demand work in tandem, and sometimes there can be a delicate balance.

The beloved Mr. Micawber addressed this type of balance in Charles Dickens' novel *David Copperfield*. Since he chose to express it in monetary terms, it seems worth repeating in a book devoted to money:

2000 Sacagawea dollar. The Anthony dollar's replacement is prettier and more popular, but is "golden" only in color, not content. *Photo courtesy United States Mint.*

"Annual income: twenty pounds, annual expenditure nineteen nineteen six, result happiness. Annual income twenty pounds, annual expenditure twenty pounds ought and six, result misery."

▶ The Impact of Hoards

Every now and then, hoards of collectible coins come to light—and when they hit the market, they can have a dramatic impact on the supply, and by extension the value, of this material. In the mid-1970's, for example, hobbyists learned that an eccentric Nevada millionaire named LaVere Redfield had died and left behind a vast hoard of coins, including more than 407,000 U.S. silver dollars of the Morgan and Peace design types. (The Morgan dollar, issued from 1878 through 1904 and again for one last time in 1921, bears a portrait of Miss Liberty and was named for its designer, U.S. Mint engraver George T. Morgan. The Peace dollar, issued intermittently from 1921 through 1935, has a modernistic likeness of Miss Liberty with rays of sunlight behind her. It was issued to mark the end of the Great War in Europe and carries the inscription "Peace" on its reverse.)

Redfield was not a collector, and simply had purchased the cartwheels at random in $1,000 bags from banks, casinos and friends, so their contents were just a representative mix of what was available when he bought them—mostly in the days when they could be obtained for little or no more than face value. Nonetheless, they did include some very scarce coins, including specimens of the 1879-CC, 1885-CC, 1893 and 1895-S Morgan dollars. They also contained a very high percentage of mint-condition coins, reflecting the fact that silver dollars never had circulated widely and most had remained in bank vaults since the time they were produced. Dealers who examined the Redfield silver dollars concluded that more than 350,000 of them were uncirculated. A-Mark Coin Co. of Beverly Hills, Calif., purchased all the coins for $7.3 million in 1976 and began dispersing them through a network of dealers.

Some voiced fear that "dumping" so many coins on the silver dollar market would depress the value of Morgan and Peace dollars as collectibles—and initially, price levels did recede. Before long, however, the temporary glut had been absorbed and prices began to advance across the board. Far from depressing the market, the Redfield coins reinforced interest in silver dollars, drawing many new collectors to the series and becoming the coins of choice for newly minted investors. The increase in supply provided by the hoard was more than offset by an even sharper subsequent rise in demand.

Morgan dollars, especially, were an ideal lure for non-collectors looking to purchase coins as an investment. They're large, hefty and impressive; each contains more than three-quarters of an ounce of precious metal; many of them were minted way back in the 1800's; and many—if not most—of them are still in mint condition. On top of that, their price tags weren't inordinately high in the late 1970's; many, in fact, undoubtedly seemed downright cheap. Market promotions, dealer manipulations and legitimate growth in demand would drive those prices considerably higher before the bubble burst in 1989. In the meantime, though, the Morgan dollar became the undisputed king of the coin market. It remains a highly popular coin, even after being dislodged from its throne—certainly much more popular than it was in the days before the 1970's, when it played second fiddle to cents, nickels and other smaller coins in the numismatic pecking order.

On the whole, hoards have been beneficial for the hobby—though not in the short term, perhaps, for individual hobbyists already holding coins of the kind contained in these accumulations. Often, hoards have preserved coins that otherwise might have been lost—at least in better condition—to future generations of collectors. That happened, for instance, in the mid-19th century when a utopian work-share commune in Economy, Pa., called the Harmony Society squirreled away a treasure trove of U.S. silver coins, many of them early silver dollars and half dollars. Researchers believe this "Economite treasure" was set aside starting in the 1830's. By one account, it contained more than $100,000 in coins when it was dug up in 1878 and sold to banks. The contents included one example of the ultrarare 1794 silver dollar and 150 specimens of the 1794 half dollar, a coin somewhat more attainable but nonetheless a recognized rarity.

Hoards of U.S. gold coins surfaced in Europe following World War II. Some had been acquired over the years by Europeans, who have long been conditioned to keep gold on hand—often under a mattress—for use in times of need. Other holdings belonged to Americans, who had shipped their coins abroad for safekeeping in European banks, and to protect them from melting, following President Roosevelt's Gold Surrender Order in 1933. Technically, the Americans could have kept their coins in American banks—or even in their homes—if the coins qualified as collectibles, for numismatic coins were exempt from the edict. Many such coins, however, were turned in just the same, either out of ignorance or out of unwillingness to risk being found in violation. By the late 1960's, large numbers of the coins had returned from Europe, for by then, American hobbyists—and speculators, too—were paying modest premiums even for common-date U.S. gold coins. The gold ownership ban was still in effect at that time, but the numismatic exemption was much better understood. The issue became moot on Dec. 31, 1974, when Americans regained their long-denied right to buy, sell and own gold bullion. Just as British numismatists had helped preserve early U.S. coinage for posterity, Europe had provided a safe haven again for millions of U.S. gold coins, many of them important collectibles, during the Americans' 40-year wandering in the precious-metal wilderness.

▶ The 'Great Silver Sale'

Even before the discovery and dispersal of the Redfield Hoard, interest in silver dollars had been stirred throughout the hobby—and beyond the hobby, too—by the federal government's sale of scarce old cartwheels found in Treasury vaults in the early 1960's. As noted in Chapter 3, these coins had been buried in the deepest recesses of the vaults and had come to light only when the Treasury cleared away the thousands of bags on top of them—using the coins in those bags to redeem silver certificates for besieging armies of opportunists.

At the time the Treasury stopped using silver dollars to redeem silver certificates, it had 2.9 million of the coins left in its vaults—most of them products of the long-closed Carson City Mint, where mintages had tended to be small. It placed these in the hands of the General Services Administration, the government's marketing arm, and GSA drafted plans for a "great silver sale" in which it would offer the coins to the American people in a series of mail-bid sales. The first of those sales opened on Oct. 31, 1972 and encompassed Carson City dollars dated 1882, 1883 and 1884. On Feb. 2, 1973, GSA announced that 700,000 coins had been sold—all for the minimum bid of $30 apiece. The sales continued—steadily at first, then sporadically—until 1980, when GSA finally sold the last of the silver dollars.

It has been suggested that the old silver dollars in the U.S. Treasury's vaults constituted the greatest coin "hoard" of all time. Treasury officials might quibble with that description—but nomenclature aside, it looked very much like a hoard and certainly had a hoard-like impact on the silver-dollar marketplace. That impact wasn't altogether positive. In fact, it was catastrophic for collectors who had purchased one particular Morgan silver dollar.

Up until the closing months of 1962, the 1903-O Morgan dollar (a coin produced in 1903 at the New Orleans Mint) was considered a great rarity and was selling for as much as $5,000—then a year's pay for most working-class Americans—in uncirculated condition. The coin's listed mintage was nearly 4.5 million, but few had ever surfaced and it was widely assumed that the vast majority had been melted during World War I—a time when many millions of U.S. silver dollars were converted into bullion and shipped to Britain. Late in 1962, bags of 1903-O silver dollars began to emerge from the Treasury's vaults as part of the inventory being used by the government to redeem silver certificates. They hadn't been melted after all. The coins' market value plummeted overnight—and when the dust settled, this former major rarity was selling for a mere $20. In time, it recovered part of its appeal and by 2001 its market value stood at $200 in typical mint condition—still a far cry from $5,000, especially considering that $5,000 in 1962 dollars would now be worth several times that amount.

The story of the 1903-O silver dollar is a cautionary tale for people buying coins. Mintage figures should never be discounted when deciding how much to pay for a given coin. Many coins have indeed been melted or otherwise lost. But if the Mint says it made 4.5 million pieces, it almost certainly did—and there's more than a little risk in gambling that all but 4.5 thousand went astray.

Coin hoards can feed market activity, but they also can jump up and bite unwary buyers in the pocketbook.

······································

Chapter 5

All About Grading

······································

No single subject has generated more controversy in the modern coin market, or had a greater impact, than grading. From the time the pendulum swung from collecting to investing during the 1970's, the prices of rare coins, the liquidity of transactions—indeed, the whole structure of the marketplace—all have hinged to a very great extent on the availability (or absence) of accurate, dependable grading.

In simplest terms, *grading* is the process of stating the condition—or level of preservation—of a coin in words and/or numbers that are readily understood by buyers and sellers. A hundred years ago, this process was far less precise—and also far less important—than it is today. That's because rarity, not quality, was then the chief determinant of value. Unless a coin was legitimately scarce, as reflected by low mintage, it would bring little or no premium—and if it *was* scarce, its value would not be appreciably higher in shiny mint condition than in circulated shape. At that time, dealers' price lists often contained just two or three grades. They might classify coins simply as "new" or "used." Or they might list prices in fine, extremely fine and uncirculated conditions. Either way, the price differentials were likely to be small. Over the years, as the market started to grow and prices began to rise at a quickened pace, intermediate grade levels came to be used—and by the 1950's, price guides such as the "Red Book" (*A Guide Book of United States Coins* by R. S. Yeoman) were showing valuations in the grades of good, very good, fine, very fine, extremely fine, about uncirculated and uncirculated. (Although "about uncirculated" is the term used in the Red Book and in the official ANA grading guide, many believe "almost uncirculated" would be a far more logical way to describe an AU coin.)

Even then, the price increments tended to be modest from grade to grade, rising arithmetically, rather than geometrically, as a coin's condition moved up the scale. Typically, the final jump to uncirculated would be somewhat greater, but uncirculated coins generally weren't viewed as a class apart—a numismatic aristocracy, as it were. They were a bit more desirable than circulated coins and a bit more expensive, but most collectors were satisfied with less and saw no compelling reason to seek out pristine specimens. A well-struck, problem-free coin in extremely fine condition—or even a grade or two less—would suffice, especially if the collector was on a budget.

There were early attempts to bring some semblance of order to coin grading, even before price differentials widened and made the need more urgent. Among the earliest was the 1958 publication of *A Guide to the Grading of United States Coins* by Martin R. Brown and John W. Dunn. The "Brown and Dunn book," as it came to be known, described grading differences in rudimentary terms and illustrated these with line drawings. Although the book enjoyed considerable success, many collectors expressed a preference for photographs over drawings—and their wish was granted in 1970 when James F. Ruddy's *Photograde* was published. As its name suggests, this book used actual photographs to show how selected coins looked in the major grade levels. This was an important step forward, but it would prove inadequate as a way of differentiating among coins within the mint-state range, once the marketplace began to recognize more specific grades and finer nuances.

▶ The Investor Mentality

The big change in grading occurred when investment came to the fore in the early to mid-1970's. A new breed of dealer was pitching rare coins to buyers with big money but very little knowledge of the numismatic field. These buyers were conditioned by their economic background to go for the biggest and best—they drove Cadillacs, not Fords, and their watches were Rolexes, not Timexes—and they brought this bias with them into buying coins. They favored large coins over small ones, gold and silver coins over copper and nickel and mint-condition coins over circulated ones. This new demand for mint-state coins drove prices sharply higher for such material. It also created a climate in which abuses flourished, for unscrupulous dealers found it easy to palm off overgraded, overpriced coins when selling to the uninitiated—and for all their professional success, most of the new investors were strictly amateurs when it came to buying coins.

The trailblazer in marketing coins primarily as investments was Stanley Apfelbaum, who established a company called First Coinvestors in Albertson, N.Y., in 1974. Apfelbaum introduced new techniques, such as telemarketing and placing ads in professional journals serving high-paying fields such as medicine and law, rather than in hobby periodicals. He was specifically targeting wealthy noncollectors, and his merchandise—like his approach—was tailored to their mind-set: "portfolios" of large, eye-catching coins in mint condition, especially Morgan dollars and Saint-Gaudens double eagles, which were really far more common than the sales pitches made it seem and often far less valuable than the prices that were attached.

First Coinvestors soon was followed by other investment-oriented companies—notably New England Rare Coin Galleries of Boston and Steve Ivy Rare Coin Co. of Dallas. Several years later, the principals of those companies, James Halperin and Steve Ivy, joined forces to establish Heritage Rare Coin Galleries of Dallas, which remains one of the industry's largest and most widely recognized dealerships as of this writing. New England Rare Coin Galleries introduced the practice of placing rare coins in self-directed retirement plans, an innovation that helped fuel the coin market boom that began in the late 1970's. Congress outlawed the practice in 1981, hastening and deepening the market's sharp decline—but up to that point, it gave investors a powerful new incentive to purchase coins.

As more and more coin dealers zeroed in on well-heeled but ill-informed investors, the prices of "investment-quality" coins rose even higher—and the abuses grew worse. The ripple effects spread throughout the marketplace, rocking collectors' boats along with those of the neophyte investors. Like the man watching his mother-in-law drive over a cliff in his new Cadillac, many collectors viewed the proceedings with mixed emotions—for while they could now get very high prices for the mint-state coins they already owned, they would find it much costlier to replace those coins in the future. Collectors and reputable dealers (who constitute the great majority in the field) had no mixed emotions, however, about the abuses being perpetrated by some of the new-look dealers. They were outraged. They also were dismayed at the lack of a coherent system of grading standards—for this was the Achilles' heel that made the abuses so easy to carry out. Vague terms such as "brilliant uncirculated," "choice uncirculated" and "gem uncirculated" were the phrases that served as "grades" at the time, and their imprecision made them almost meaningless.

▶ The ANA Takes the Lead

The American Numismatic Association seemed a logical choice to lead the coin market out of the grading wilderness. In 1972, the ANA had successfully tackled another serious problem—the proliferation of counterfeit and altered coins—by establishing the ANA Certification Service (ANACS), which examined coins submitted for its review to determine if they were genuine. By the mid-1970's, ANACS had made significant strides toward downsizing that problem from a crisis to just a nuisance, and members—dealers as well as collectors—were urging it to tackle the grading problem next.

The ANA accepted the challenge, appointing a committee headed by Abe Kosoff, one of the country's most respected coin dealers, to draft grading standards that would be readily used and accepted throughout the industry. Kosoff and his panel came up with a recommendation that in retrospect seems ill-advised. They proposed a grading system based on the 1-to-70 scale already in use to denote the condition of large cents—the copper one-cent pieces issued by the U.S. Mint from 1793 through 1857. The system had been devised in 1949 by Dr. William H. Sheldon, a well-known specialist in these coins, who described it at the time as "a quantitative grading of condition."

Sheldon had observed that the 1794 cent, one of the most popular and sought after coins in the series, was selling for about a dollar in the lowest collectible condition. He therefore established $1 as the *basal value* in his system and assigned a grade of 1 to coins in that condition. Since examples graded *good* were selling for $4 each, he gave these a numerical grade of 4. He continued up the scale, in each case assigning a grade that corresponded to the current market value of a 1794 cent in that condition. In this manner, he arrived at grades, or grade ranges, of 7 to 10 for *very good,* 12 to 15 for *fine,* 20 to 30 for *very fine,* 40 for *extremely fine,* 50 for *about uncirculated* and 60 to 70 for *mint state.*

In adapting the Sheldon scale, the ANA viewed it as a known commodity with which many dealers and collectors already were familiar, but its shortcomings far outweighed any perceived advantages. Its primary weakness was the fact that it compressed all mint-state coins into the narrow range from 60 to 70—for while this represented only about one-seventh of the scale, mint-state coins accounted for the great majority of the ones for which grades were being sought. A 1-to-100 scale with 20, 25 or even 50 grades for mint-state coins would have been far more logical—and its decimal basis would have made grading determinations far simpler.

The ANA promulgated its standards in a 1977 book called *Official A.N.A. Grading Standards for United States Coins,* written by Ken Bressett and Abe Kosoff. Two years later, in March 1979, ANACS began grading coins according to these standards. Initially, its work was warmly welcomed; the coin market was in the midst of its greatest boom in history, and the rocket got extra propulsion from newfound confidence in grading. Within a few years, however, the bloom was off the rose—and the rise was off the boom: The coin market tumbled following the collapse of gold and silver bullion, and ANACS grading came under much closer scrutiny. As prices fell, so did confidence in the new grading system. Critics complained that it was inaccurate, inconsistent and irrelevant to the marketplace. Increasingly, they carped that ANA was using an academic approach to grading, rather than relating it to the real world of flesh-and-blood buyers and sellers.

◗ The Grading Revolution

By the mid-1980's, disenchantment with ANACS grading had reached the point where many in the marketplace were almost in open revolt against the system. Just as the ferment was reaching full boil, a group of leading dealers announced an undertaking that calmed the crisis virtually overnight. The group, headed by West Coast dealer David Hall, had established a company called the Professional Coin Grading Service (PCGS, for short) that would grade coins in a new way calculated to reassure the marketplace. Its graders would all be dealers who had spent their time on bourse floors, not in ivory towers, and grades would be determined through a process of consensus: Three different experts would assign a grade to each coin, and a fourth expert then would "finalize" the grade by ratifying the majority opinion. Beyond the grading itself, PCGS would encapsulate each coin in a sonically sealed, hard plastic holder along with an insert setting forth its grade. This would provide protection for both the coin itself and the statement of its grade, deterring potential tampering. ANACS, by contrast, had signified its findings in the form of photo certificates and hadn't sealed coins after grading them.

Another important distinction was that PCGS would assign a single grade to each coin, while ANACS often used split grading when one side of a coin was better than the other. Thus, ANACS might have described a coin as MS-67/63 if its obverse was MS-67 but its reverse was only MS-63. At PCGS, the same coin might be graded MS-65, taking the average overall condition of the two sides—or perhaps only MS-64, or even MS-63, if its experts concluded that the weaker side set the tone in determining the coin's market value. Unfortunately, PCGS retained the 1-to-70 grading scale, reasoning that this was by then well

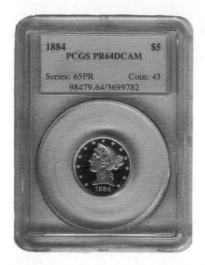

1884 Liberty half eagle in PCGS holder. This $5 gold piece received a grade of Proof-64 Deep Cameo. *Photos courtesy Scott A. Travers/PCGS.*

established. Notwithstanding this, the company truly launched a revolution in grading.

PCGS began operations in February 1986 in Newport Beach, Calif. Within a year, it had a major competitor when one of its founders, John Albanese, left to establish a new grading service called the Numismatic Guaranty Corporation of America (NGC) in Parsippany, N.J. (NGC moved to Sarasota, Fla., in 2000.) Albanese objected to the fact that PCGS permitted its principals and employees to deal in coins. This was not allowed at NGC. Otherwise, NGC paralleled PCGS in most respects, using a similar consensus form of arm's-length third-party grading and encapsulating coins in hard plastic holders after they were certified. These holders, from whatever service, came to be known informally as "slabs" from the very outset.

The American Numismatic Association continued to operate ANACS until 1989, when it sold its coin-grading operation to

Amos Press of Sidney, Ohio, publisher of *Coin World* and other hobby periodicals. The new owner relocated the operation to Columbus, Ohio, and retained the name ANACS—although the ANA no longer had a role in the enterprise. Since that time, ANACS has maintained a presence in the coin-grading business, although on a much smaller scale than PCGS and NGC. Other companies also have carved out niches—notably the Independent Coin Grading Company (ICG) of Littleton, Colo., which was founded in 1998. But PCGS and NGC have been the main players, with PCGS generally perceived as Number One and NGC as its main rival.

The Elements of Grading

In determining the grade of a coin, the certification services consider a number of factors. They may differ in the way they judge each of these elements, but all of them use the same general checklist in arriving at their conclusions. Some of these may have more relevance to mint-state coins, but all can come into play even with circulated coins.

The principal elements are:

- ▶ **The presence or absence of marks.** This consideration is particularly important with mint-state coins. Scratches, gouges, hairlines and other imperfections can drastically reduce the grade and value of a coin, especially if they occur in open parts of the design, where they are more obvious.
- ▶ **The degree of luster.** Collectors prefer coins that reflect light evenly and pleasingly. Bright, uniform surfaces enhance a coin's grade, while a dark, uneven appearance is a detriment.
- ▶ **The sharpness of the strike.** Well-struck coins with sharp detail are far more appealing to collectors than "weak

strikes," where much of the design may look blurry and indistinct. A weakly struck coin can still receive a mint-state grade if the weakness does indeed stem from a production flaw, rather than wear.

▶ **The kind of toning.** Some collectors favor brilliant mint-state coins; others are partial to coins with technicolor toning. At various times the grading services, too, have shown a preference for one or the other through the grades they have assigned.

▶ **The level of eye appeal.** This is really a cumulative element representing the combined effect of all the others. It also is perhaps the most subjective factor—for unlike marks and sharpness, for example, eye appeal can't be quantified.

With certain coins, other factors also may be important. In grading mint-state copper coins, for instance, the services normally designate whether they are RD (fully red), RB (red and brown) or BN (totally brown). Red coins are considered the most desirable and bring the highest premiums. Special designations also are used, when applicable, for Standing Liberty quarters with full heads (FH), "Mercury" dimes with full split bands in the fasces (FSB) and Franklin half dollars with full bell lines in the Liberty Bell (FBL). Some coins, particularly Morgan silver dollars, also may be designated prooflike (PL), deep-mirror prooflike (DMPL) or cameo (CM). These added descriptions enhance the coins' grade and value, for they indicate positive features such as greater sharpness of strike and eye appeal.

Within the 11-grade range allotted for mint-state coins, certain grades have special significance. MS-65, for example, is the threshold at which coins begin to be viewed as superior specimens and unusually desirable. This grade might be likened to the base camp from which mountain climbers launch their final ascent to the top of Mount Everest—with Everest in this case being MS-70, which represents absolute perfection. Any grade above MS-65 is in a rarefied zone, and this is reflected in very substantial premiums in the marketplace. As a rule, investors prefer to limit their purchases to coins graded at least MS-65.

Proof coins normally do not circulate, and thus in most cases their grades parallel those of mint-state coins. A proof coin meriting a grade of 65 would be designated Proof-65. Proof coins with wear or other detractions that render them less than uncirculated are given grades that correspond to business-strike coins in the same levels. A Proof-40 coin, for example, is in the same condition as an extremely fine business strike.

How to Grade Coins

The average collector—and even the average dealer—can't expect to master the intricacies of coin grading to the same extent as the experts at PCGS, NGC and the other services. It is possible, however, to attain a reasonably high degree of proficiency—high enough to function without relying exclusively on certified grading as a crutch. This can be a valuable skill, for certification isn't infallible and being able to grade with relative accuracy provides an important safety net when the system falls down on the job. The key to good grading is to "systematize the process, so as not to be overwhelmed by any single characteristic," according to Scott A. Travers, who provides a detailed, step-by-step description of how to grade coins in *The Coin Collector's Survival Manual, Fourth Edition* (Bonus Books, Chicago, 2000).

The first step in grading a coin is to grip it tightly between your thumb and forefinger over a soft surface, such as a velvet cloth (in case you inadvertently drop the coin). Always hold coins by the edge; touching their surface with an oily fingertip can leave an unsightly blemish that will permanently reduce their grade level

Left, *1880 Morgan dollar graded Mint State-67.* This coin is sharply struck and virtually flawless.
Center, *1881-CC Morgan dollar graded Mint State-65.* This coin has a few small flaws, but not in grade-sensitive areas.
Right, *1879 Morgan dollar graded Mint State-60.* This coin has numerous nicks and scratches, but no signs of circulation wear. *Photos courtesy Scott A. Travers/NGC PhotoProof.*

and their value. Holding the coin under a pinpoint light source, you should tilt and rotate it so you can see it from every angle. Looking first at the obverse (or "heads" side), scan the coin clockwise (counterclockwise if you're left-handed) until you've covered the entire surface. Then turn the coin over and examine the reverse in the same manner. Some people like to divide the coin mentally into quadrants, like pieces of a pie, to simplify this process and ensure that they don't miss anything. Finally, look at the "third side" of the coin—its edge. Throughout this examination, you should consider the elements listed in the previous section—marks (or their absence), luster, strike, toning and eye appeal.

The difference between one mint-state grade and the next-higher—or next-lower—grade can be subtle and difficult for any-

Left, *1908 Saint-Gaudens double eagle graded Mint State-68.*
Impeccable, shimmering surfaces stamp this as a nearly perfect coin.
Center, *1927 Saint-Gaudens double eagle graded Mint State-65.* There
are tiny nicks on this coin, but they don't detract significantly.
Right, *1909 Saint-Gaudens double eagle graded Mint State-62.*
Although it has no wear, this coin's numerous blemishes make it an inferior
uncirculated specimen. *Photos courtesy Scott A. Travers/PCGS.*

one other than experts to discern. Normally, though, it is fairly
easy to differentiate between coins that are separated by two or
more mint-state levels. This becomes evident upon examination of
the two sets of accompanying photographs. One set illustrates the
obverses of three Morgan silver dollars certified in the grades of
Mint State-67, Mint State-65 and Mint State-60. The other shows
the obverses of three Saint-Gaudens double eagles graded MS-68,
MS-65 and MS-62. The MS-67 silver dollar and MS-68 double
eagle are both sharply struck and virtually free from imperfections.
The MS-65 coins are *relatively* well struck and *relatively* free from
flaws—and, most important, they have no nicks, marks or scratches
in grade-sensitive areas, such as Miss Liberty's broad, flat cheek on
the silver dollar. The MS-60 silver dollar and MS-62 double eagle

both have obvious flaws, though neither displays wear and both thus qualify as uncirculated coins.

PCGS provided a detailed description of its grading standards in a 1997 book called the *Official Guide to Coin Grading and Coun-*

---

lines will be sharp. The minor devices/lettering around the periphery will be clear. **Note:** For some series (Barber coinage, in particular), there will be slight wear into the reverse rim that touches some letters.

MARKS: There can be some minor marks, but major ones will be worn away.

EYE APPEAL: Any eye appeal will be due to clean surfaces and lack of marks.

G-4 Morgan dollar obverse. The head is worn mostly smooth, with only slight detail in the recessed areas. The rim is worn through the dentils and is slightly blended into the field.

G-4 Morgan dollar reverse. The eagle is worn smooth with only slight detail seen in the lower wing feathers. The wreath will show slight detail. The rim is worn through most of the dentils and into the field.

G-4: Good

WEAR: Only the outlines of the major devices are still visible. The minor devices/lettering around the periphery will be worn but still clear. **Note:** For some series (Barber coinage, in particular), there will be some wear into the top parts of the reverse lettering.

MARKS: There may be marks, but they should not be severe.

EYE APPEAL: Virtually no eye appeal, but nice, even wear can be pleasing to the eye.

AG-3: About Good

WEAR: The wear will be considerable, with the rims mostly gone, sometimes blending with devices.

MARKS: There may be numerous marks, but usually the surfaces are smooth from wear.

AG-3 Morgan dollar obverse. The head is worn very smooth, with only LIBERTY and a few recessed areas, such as the ear, still showing detail. The rims are worn through all of the dentils and into the stars and lettering.

EYE APPEAL: None.

FR-2: Fair

WEAR: There will only be partial device detail visible. The date can be weak or almost missing. The rims may be completely worn.

MARKS: There may be numerous marks, but usually the surfaces are smooth from wear.

EYE APPEAL: None.

AG-3 Morgan dollar reverse. The eagle is very flat, with slight wing feather detail present. The wreath is outlined, but shows no detail. The rims are worn into the tops of the lettering.

FR-2 Morgan dollar obverse. There is almost no detail seen on the head, but LIBERTY is still clear, as it is deeply recessed. The rims are worn deeply into the lettering and touch the date and stars.

FR-2 Morgan dollar reverse. Slight lower wing detail is seen, though the eagle is worn very flat. The rims are worn deeply into all of the peripheral lettering.

PO-1: Poor

WEAR: The amount of wear is so massive that sometimes only the date and a few details are visible. If the date is not visible, the coin can be graded only if it is a one-year type.

PO-1 Morgan dollar obverse. Heavy wear is seen, with the rims deeply worn into the field. The date is discernible.

PO-1 Morgan dollar reverse. Only the central area still has detail. The reverse may be worn nearly smooth on some specimens.

A page from the PCGS grading guide. This shows how to grade coins in circulated condition. *Photo courtesy Scott A. Travers/PCGS.*

terfeit Detection (House of Collectibles, New York). The text is accompanied by extensive illustrations. The PCGS grading book and other grading and price guides are examined in Books For Further Reading at the end of this book.

▶ After the Revolution

The grading revolution triggered by PCGS in 1986 set the stage for another market boom. It not only restored full confidence in the market among existing participants but also caught the eye of important new ones—including Wall Street brokerage houses looking to expand their investment horizons. Demand soared especially for mint-state "generic" coins—high-grade examples of certified common-date coins in flashy, glitzy series such as Morgan dollars, Saint-Gaudens double eagles and Walking Liberty half dollars. These appealed to Wall Street because, like stocks and bonds, they could be traded readily in interchangeable units. But in 1989, the sizzle turned to fizzle as Wall Street got cold feet and certified generic coins—highly overpriced in terms of their real rarity—plummeted in value, sending many investors to the sidelines.

The exodus of investors was hastened when a very powerful "camel"—the Federal Trade Commission—poked its nose under the coin market's tent. The FTC took action in the late 1980's against several coin companies that it accused of fraudulent practices. Its efforts in this regard were welcomed by many dealers and collectors as a major step toward cleaning up the marketplace, even though they hurt legitimate businesses as well by shaking buyers' confidence. Some took exception, however, when the FTC also trained its heavy ammunition on PCGS, accusing the company of deceptive and misleading practices. Although the charges sounded sweeping and serious, the alleged violations were actually quite technical and relatively minor. By tarring such a key player in the coin industry with such a broad brush, the FTC inflicted major and lasting damage on the coin market as a whole. PCGS signed a consent decree in which it agreed not to engage in the alleged violations but admitted to no wrongdoing.

With investors largely gone, the grading services reinvented themselves to meet the new realities. They started grading foreign and ancient coins to shore up their sagging volume. They modified their fees to help attract more submissions. They introduced innovations such as NGC's "Photo Proof" program, which offers word-and-picture stories of the coins being certified. They encouraged certification of very high-grade modern coins. And they launched "registry" programs to give collectors incentive to acquire high-grade coins and have them certified. These measures helped the major grading companies weather the transition from the investor era of the 1980's to collector domination during the 1990's and beyond.

▶ Grading the Graders

At first glance, PCGS and NGC may look like Tweedle-Dee and Tweedle-Dum. Their operations are similar, both serve essentially the same clientele and both enjoy broad acceptance in the marketplace. On closer examination, though, there are important differences. The most important differences involve the strictness and consistency of their grading. Although they strive to create the impression that their standards never change, both in fact have modified those standards, or at least applied them differently, at various times through the years—sometimes becoming stricter, other times more liberal, usually in response to market conditions. Early on, NGC grading was widely viewed as stricter than that of PCGS, and NGC-graded coins tended to command somewhat higher premiums than PCGS coins in the same grade. Basically, the marketplace concluded that the NGC pieces were better coins. More recently, NGC grading came to be perceived as somewhat looser and PCGS coins began to bring higher prices in many instances.

Both services are respected, and many coins from both companies enjoy a high degree of liquidity—that is to say, they change hands readily at (and sometimes far above) the levels in the authoritative *Certified Coin Dealer Newsletter*, the so-called "Bluesheet," which tracks sight-unseen dealer "bids" for certified coins every week. All too often, though, dealers with loose standards of their own will sell consumers NGC coins at PCGS prices at times when there is a meaningful gap between their market values—or vice versa, at times when NGC coins are bringing higher prices. Coins from the two services often do bring similar prices, but at other times there can be significant variation—sometimes amounting to thousands of dollars on higher-priced material. The marketplace dictates values, and in that respect, coins from the two services are definitely not interchangeable.

One easy way to compare grading standards of PCGS- and NGC-certified coins is to monitor the Certified Coin Market Indicator in the Bluesheet's sister publication, the *Coin Dealer Newsletter* (or "Greysheet"). This is an index based on the Bluesheet's sight-unseen bids and compares certified coins that have been given the same grades by different services. The index uses the current bids for commonly traded *uncertified* coins as listed in the *Coin Dealer Newsletter* as its benchmark and compares dealer sight-unseen bids for certified coins of different services.

As of Jan. 25, 2002, the Certified Coin Market Indicator showed PCGS with a percentage of 86.03 for Morgan dollars and NGC with a percentage of 81.81. In other words, if a certain Morgan dollar was bid at $100 in the Greysheet, a PCGS-certified example of that coin had an average dealer sight-unseen bid of $86.03 and an NGC-graded specimen had an average sight-unseen bid of $81.81. That's close, but the difference would be enough to buy a good cigar. Other grading services trailed well behind in the comparisons.

An Expert's Opinions

John Albanese, who helped establish PCGS and then founded NGC, is uniquely qualified to grade the graders, so to speak—and is now in a position to take an arm's-length view of the industry as a whole, since he no longer has a financial stake in any grading service. Albanese candidly acknowledges that when he was grading coins, he based his judgments not on any hard-and-fast permanent standards set up by the two companies, but rather on how much each coin should bring in the marketplace at the time.

"I always market-graded coins," he declared, "and I would think that other graders did the same. I would pick up a Saint-Gaudens double eagle, for example, and say, 'This is an $800 coin.' And then I would assign the grade that corresponded to $800 at that particular time. In other words, I started with the value and worked back to the grade, rather than the other way around."

This flies in the face of grading services' long-standing claims that their standards remain constant over time. It also helps explain why coins graded, say, MS-65 during a boom market may be a point level—or even several point levels—better than coins of the same type that receive the same grade when the market is depressed. With this in mind, insiders seek out slabbed coins that were certified during the services' earliest years, when the market was strong, then "crack" the coins out of their holders and resubmit them in the hope—and expectation—of getting an upgrade.

▶ Online 'Registry' Programs

As of January 2002, Albanese said, grading standards at PCGS and NGC had been "stable" since 1995. He voiced serious con-

cern, however, about the "registry" programs then being conducted by the two services. These programs seemed harmless
enough at first blush: To encourage collectors to submit their
coins for certification, PCGS established a "Set Registry Program"—accessible at its computer Web site—at the beginning of
2001 listing the finest known collections of PCGS-certified
coins, as determined by the overall average grades of their com-
ponents. This appealed to collectors' competitive spirit, and soon
they were vying to upgrade their coins in order to gain a listing
in the registry. Seeing how popular this program quickly
became, NGC launched a registry of its own in June 2001, with
the difference that this one listed collections containing both
NGC- and PCGS-certified coins.

By the end of 2001, the programs had stirred enormous interest—more, perhaps, than the grading services had anticipated. They
also had triggered a buying spree involving modern coins in exceptional condition. By the summer of 2001, normally conservative
collectors were paying thousands of dollars for common-date Lincoln cents and other modern coins which had been certified in very
high grade levels—with the sole objective of gaining recognition in
one of the online registries. In one case, a 1954-P Lincoln cent
graded MS-67 RD by PCGS sold for $3,600 because it was the only
example certified up to then in such a high condition. The 1954-P
cent has a mintage of nearly 72 million and is readily available for 50
cents in MS-63 condition and less than $2 in MS-65 RD. Even in
the grade of MS-66 RD, it was selling at the time for only about $30.

Albanese maintains that this type of frenzy is dangerous to the
financial health of the people paying such prices. More than that,
he's concerned that it could be bad for the hobby as a whole—and
the grading services in particular—in the long run.

"I think there's 100-percent certainty that these coins will
come down in value," he remarked. "In reality, they already have

come down—but no one is trying to sell them, so no one knows it yet. If you take a $1,000 1964 half dollar or a $1,000 1945 penny and go out and try to sell it to a knowledgeable dealer, you'll get an offer of $5 or $10. People are paying these prices on the basis that these are the only coins listed in these particular grades in the PCGS Population Report and the NGC Census Report. But that doesn't mean they're the only ones in existence; it just means that nobody else ever bothered to send them in because they didn't think it was worthwhile.

"When I started out at NGC, no one would ever send a 1945 penny to be graded. Now all of a sudden, because of registry sets and modern coin promotions on the Internet or on TV home-shopping channels, they're beginning to be submitted. Obviously, the first few that are graded MS-67 or higher will have low populations—but two or three years down the road, there could be a thousand of those coins graded MS-67."

In Albanese's view, certified grading is unwarranted, for the most part, for any U.S. coins dated after 1964 and for any Lincoln cents after 1945, with the exception of major mint-error coins such as the 1955 and 1972 doubled-die cents.

▶ Population and Census Reports

The PCGS Population Report is a monthly publication detailing the number of coins the company has certified for each date and mint in every U.S. series, with a breakdown listing the number in each grade level. The NGC Census Report is a similar publication, likewise issued monthly. Both are intended to guide collectors and dealers by showing at a glance the relative scarcity—and availability—of coins in the most commonly traded grades, especially within the mint-state range. Many buyers and sellers do, in fact, give heavy weight to the "pop report" figures when deciding how much to pay for certain coins—particularly those in the very highest grades.

Unfortunately, the figures are often unreliable and sometimes downright misleading. As already noted in regard to "registry" programs, low population figures for very high-grade examples of common-date modern coins may not reflect true rarity, but rather the fact that very few examples have been submitted—simply because hardly anyone considered it worthwhile to do so and to pay the certification fees for coins with such massive mintages. This comes into play not only with registry sets, but also when very high-grade modern coins (including American Eagle bullion coins) are offered for sale on TV home-shopping networks. The hucksters on these channels make a big fuss about the coins' low populations in the grading service reports—but it's altogether possible that they're the only ones that have bothered to submit them for certification.

At the other extreme, some listings in the population and census reports actually *overstate* the number of coins submitted and *understate* their rarity because of a practice known as "resubmissions." Because a one-grade difference frequently may result in a price differential of thousands—even tens of thousands—of dollars for truly rare coins, there is powerful incentive to "crack" a coin out of its holder if it receives the lower grade, then send it back to the service for regrading and possible upgrading to the higher level. PCGS and NGC both list each submission—including resubmissions of the same exact coin—in their monthly reports, as if each one involved a different coin. Thus, a report may show a rare coin with a population of 15 in a given grade when, in fact, 10 of those may represent the same coin. This has the effect of making the coin appear less rare—and less valuable—than it really is in that condition.

▶ 'Doctored' Coins

Simply resubmitting coins and counting on the graders to view them more optimistically the second (or twenty-second) time around isn't exactly a surefire formula for success. The graders have good memories, especially when it comes to rare and distinctive coins, and soon catch on when they see the same material over and over. Realizing this, some submitters take matters into their own hands by altering—and seeking to enhance—the appearance of coins through artificial toning, chemical etching and other techniques.

Some "coin doctors" have mastered their black arts to the point where they can fool the grading services every now and then. Given the large price differentials involved, getting a coin graded one level—or even two or three levels—above its actual condition can make this arcane practice well worthwhile financially. Innocent victims who later buy such coins at least have the protection of the major services' buy-back guarantee: In the event a doctored coin deteriorated after being "slabbed," the services would purchase it at the current market value of the same coin in the grade at which it was certified.

▶ Final Thoughts on Grading

On balance, third-party grading has been a positive force in the rare-coin marketplace. It stabilized the market at a time when chaos reigned, and over the years it has furnished a viable framework for buying and selling coins "sight-unseen"—without physically seeing them prior to consummating a sale. By and large, the grading has been pretty much on the money—especially at PCGS and NGC—and while it hasn't always been as accurate and consistent as dealers, collectors and the grading services themselves would like, it also hasn't fluctuated wildly.

Many collectors chafed at the notion of encapsulating coins when that practice was instituted—and some still do—because it places a barrier between themselves and their coins, making it impossible to hold them and admire them up close and personal. Old-timers will probably never accept this unwelcome intrusion upon their collecting enjoyment. On the other hand, truly rare coins are much more valuable now than in the good old days, and the hard plastic holders are a sturdy form of protection and preservation.

The grading system introduced in 1986 and refined since that time isn't perfect, but it's better by far than the one that it replaced. It would be even better if the 1-to-70 grading scale somehow could be scrapped and replaced with a more logical and manageable system. That seems unlikely, however, given the fact that millions of coins already have been certified and encapsulated under the existing system.

▶ How to Submit Coins for Grading

At one time, PCGS and NGC accepted coin submissions only from authorized dealers, and individuals with coins to be certified had to submit them through one of these dealers. As of this writing in February 2002, both will accept direct submissions from individual collectors or other interested parties under certain circumstances. PCGS now accepts submissions either through authorized dealers or directly from PCGS Collectors Club members. NGC accepts submissions through authorized dealer/members, or directly from members of its Certified Collectors Society or the American Numismatic Association. NGC is the official grading service of the ANA. At both PCGS and NGC, the fee is $15 per coin for "economy" service, which involves a turnaround time of about a month. Faster service is available for higher fees.

For detailed information on how to submit coins, contact PCGS at (800) 447-8848 or NGC at (800) NGC-COIN. Their mailing addresses are:

PCGS
P.O. Box 9458
Newport Beach, CA 92658

NGC
P.O. Box 4776
Sarasota, FL 34230

Chapter 6

Caveat Emptor

Authentication and grading by impartial third-party services have greatly reduced the risk once posed by counterfeit and altered coins and also curtailed abuses stemming from overgrading. Fast-buck artists have other effective weapons at their disposal, however—and far from leaving the coin market in the wake of the grading revolution, they have simply devised new ways (or variations on old ways) to fleece the unwary. In some instances, they have even utilized some of the protections built into third-party certification to give their new rip-offs an air of legitimacy.

The rare coin market can be a perilous place for those who spend large sums of money without first taking at least a little time to learn the lay of the land. It also is a place where having a little knowledge can indeed be a dangerous thing—for that tends to create a false sense of security that can lead to costly mistakes. There are better protections for coin buyers today than in earlier generations, but there also are higher stakes—and greater risks— because many rare coins are much more expensive than in the past and big swings in price often hinge on small differentials in grade.

▶ Rip-Offs of the Past

As objects with value, coins have always had a natural attraction for those seeking ill-gotten gains. Outright theft of another's money is the simplest way to obtain such gains, of course—and Shakespeare to the contrary, "who steals my purse" can sometimes steal a great deal more than trash. Over the centuries, though, swindlers have devised some much more imaginative ways to relieve other people of their money—sometimes by using money itself as their weapon.

1883 "No-Cents" Liberty Head nickel. Fast-buck artists gold-plated this coin and passed it off as a $5 gold piece because it lacked the word "Cents." *Photos courtesy Krause Publications.*

▶ In 1883, the U.S. Mint introduced a new five-cent piece, the Liberty Head nickel, and con men quickly seized upon a small but significant flaw in its design. The Mint's chief engraver, Charles E. Barber, had failed to include the word "Cents," denoting the value only by the large Roman numeral "V" (for "five"). Sharpies discovered that by gold-plating the coin, which was not yet familiar to much of the American public, they could pass it off as a $5 gold piece. The two denominations were almost identical in diameter—and though $5 gold pieces were considerably heavier, many retail employees didn't have much experience in handling gold coins. When word of the fraudulent practice reached the Mint, it immediately added "Cents" to the design—correcting the problem but offering little solace to those who had already been nicked for a $4.95 loss.

"With-Cents" Liberty Head nickel reverse. The word "Cents" was added partway through production in 1883. *Photo courtesy Krause Publications.*

▶ In the early 1960's, with late-date U.S. proof sets all the rage, a market developed for unopened Mint-sealed sets—and helped open the way for another form of fraud. At that time, each proof set contained five coins (the cent, nickel, dime, quarter and half dollar) housed in a flexible Phofilm (soft plastic) sheet which, in turn, was inserted in a small brown kraft-paper envelope. This envelope was sealed, much like any other mail, and the so-called "flat-pack" set was sent to the buyer. In 1960, some proof sets contained the scarce "small-date" version of that year's Lincoln cent, giving lucky recipients a valuable bonus. Partly with that in mind and partly from a belief that unexamined proof sets were less likely to be "picked over," some buyers began demanding sealed sets when they bought them in the resale market. This provided an opening for rip-off artists: They steamed open proof set envelopes, replaced the coins with washers of equal weight, then resealed them and sold them to fastidious—and very foolish—victims. Some of those envelopes still may lie unopened, gathering dust—but not a dime of value—in their owners' safe deposit boxes.

▶ In a variation on the same scam, and during the same time period, unscrupulous sellers exploited the fast-paced market in rolls of modern U.S. coins by salting rolls of higher-priced coins with similar but less valuable pieces of the same denomination. They would place examples of the scarcer coin—a 1950-D Jefferson nickel, for instance—at the ends of each roll, then fill the middle with more common pieces, such as the relatively inexpensive 1950 nickel from Philadelphia. Naturally, they would charge the going price for a roll of 40 low-mintage 1950-D nickels—$1,000 or more at the height of the market—even though most of the coins were worth far less.

▶ Sunday Supplement Specials

The magazine and comics sections of Sunday newspapers have long been a popular advertising medium for mail-order coin dealers—as well as stamp dealers—seeking to reach a wide audience. It was through such ads that B. Max Mehl, one of the biggest and best coin dealers of his day, built and maintained his business between the 1920's and the mid-1950's. Like P. T. Barnum, Mehl was a showman but a reputable one, and today he is enshrined in the Hall of Fame of the American Numismatic Association, the nation's largest coin club. More recently, this venue has been used on a regular basis by other coin dealerships that have enjoyed good reputations in the marketplace, including one of the country's highest-volume coin sellers, Littleton Coin Company of Littleton, N.H.

Unfortunately, Sunday supplements also have been prime hunting grounds for companies hawking coins of dubious value for prices that range from excessive to downright exorbitant. Their ads have become more frequent—and sometimes more flagrant—in recent years, apparently because of the heightened interest in coins generated by the 50 State Quarters Program. The general American public is more aware of coins than in the past, and hucksters have used this entrée to shill a variety of "specials" that are anything but special in terms of providing good value.

Some of these advertisers wrap themselves in an undeserved mantle of respectability—no doubt in an effort to overcome readers' defense mechanisms—by giving themselves names that sound highly official and even quasi-governmental. "Federal," "National," "American," "Washington," "Trust" and "Mint"—these are among the words that appear in such companies' names. There's nothing illegal about this, but it raises a red warning flag for knowledgeable coin hobbyists—one that all too often proves to be justified by the nature of the deals being offered.

As the new millennium approached, Sunday-supplement coin ads frequently were tied to this milestone in human history. Readers were urged to acquire the last U.S. silver dollar—or last $5 gold piece, or whatever—of the old century (and, by extension, the old millennium). While others argued whether the real start of the new millennium was Jan. 1, 2000 or Jan. 1, 2001, these ads appeared to regard it as a movable feast: At first they treated 2000 as the first year of the 21st century—then, when 2000 arrived, they shifted gears and announced that 2001 was the real beginning, giving themselves a whole new group of "last-year" collectibles to promote.

One ad from Group A—pegged to 2000 as the start of the new century—offered readers a chance to obtain the "Last Silver Dollar of the Millennium." The ad went on to audaciously proclaim it "the most anticipated coin in numismatic history." That elephantine build-up brought forth a mouse: The coin, it turned out, was the 1999 American Eagle silver bullion coin—colorized in red, white and blue and, for good measure, a splash of yellow. For starters, many (this author included) did not consider 1999 the last year of the old millennium. Beyond that, while this coin might technically be described as a "silver dollar" because it is silver and has a face value of $1, collectors normally apply that term only to regular-issue coins such as Morgan dollars—and they do not consider standard American Eagles to be numismatic, making it unlikely that this particular coin would have any place at all in "numismatic history."

As usual, however, the worst news was waiting at the bottom line: At a time when American Eagle silver bullion coins were selling for less than $7 apiece, the advertiser was asking nearly six times as much—$39.95 each—for this greatly "anticipated" coin, not counting $3.95 for shipping and handling. True, it was colorized, transforming it (in the ad's rapturous prose) into "a coin of lasting beauty and intrinsic value." While that no doubt increased the seller's cost somewhat, it did nothing to enhance the coin's value in the eyes of most numismatists, who view such an alteration as a detriment, not a bonus. As for intrinsic value—well yes, it will always be worth the spot price of an ounce of silver bullion—probably minus a discount for the coloring.

Around the same time, another newspaper ad gave readers a truly golden opportunity: A chance to acquire "the last American $5 gold coin of the century." Again, the coin in question was an American Eagle bullion coin—this time the smallest fractional gold piece, which contains one-tenth of an ounce of gold and carries a face value of $5. The seller proudly announced that "for a limited time," it would furnish this "carefully die struck" coin, "an exquisite Brilliant Uncirculated Collectors Piece," for "just $59.00"—plus $4.50 postage and handling. Lucky buyers could "save" even more by purchasing multiple examples—up to and including a "Banker's Roll" of 50 pieces for $2,450. At $49 apiece, they could thereby "save $625.00," and to make that deal even sweeter, the coins would be delivered postpaid.

At the time the ad appeared in the summer of 1999, the tenth-ounce American Eagle was selling for $32 apiece. That included the markup for fabrication and distribution. Gold bullion was trading in a narrow range around $260 an ounce, so the $5 American Eagle contained only $26 worth of gold. At $59 apiece, the advertiser's price was almost twice as high as what the coin would have cost at coin shops all around the country. Patrons of those coin shops could have obtained a roll of 50 pieces for $1,600— probably less, with the volume discount available from coin dealers, if not bankers. So even after the $625 "saving" for buying in bulk, plus the free postage, anyone accepting this offer would have ended up paying 50 percent more than the going market price— almost $500 an ounce at a time when gold was selling for only $260 an ounce.

Similar offers—sometimes the very same ones—appear from time to time as inserts in the monthly statements sent out by credit-card companies. Getting such an offer with a credit-card bill is tantamount to being placed in double jeopardy—for credit-card debt is demonstrably unwise and using high-interest credit cards to buy low-value coins is a long step down the road to financial perdition.

▶ Home Shopping Networks

The dismal values offered in many of the Sunday-supplement coin ads are bargains by comparison with some of the deals on shop-at-home cable-TV networks. While the newspaper ads frequently resort to screaming headlines, they're low-key—even dignified—next to the nonstop barkers who hawk those TV wares like madcap magpies. These shameless shills seem almost comical as they vie to top each other in lavishing undeserved praise on the grossly over-priced products they purvey. There's nothing funny, though, about the heavy losses the purchasers of these items will suffer down the line when they try to sell them. Clearly, large numbers of unin-formed—and unsuspecting—victims are snapping up these deals, for without substantial sales the coin segments would have been discontinued long ago.

Among the coin items offered regularly on home shopping networks are modern U.S. proof sets, American Eagle gold and sil-ver bullion coins, type sets of circulated U.S. coins from the early and middle 1900's and certified examples of common-date silver and gold coins such as Morgan silver dollars and Saint-Gaudens double eagles ($20 gold pieces). All of these are readily available—which of course is a prerequisite for mass marketing—and all lend themselves to price manipulation that is difficult for novices to detect. Just as important, all make a nice appearance, seeming thereby to ratify the steady stream of superlatives heaped upon them by the programs' hosts.

On one segment that aired on a home shopping network in January 2002, the two male hosts were peddling a group of proof sets from the 1960's—one for each year in the decade, with Special Mint Sets being substituted for the three years (1965 through 1967) when proof sets weren't made by the U.S. Mint. This is pedestrian fare with a broad collector base but a less than stellar record in the marketplace. To hear the hosts describe it, though, it was one of the greatest buying opportunities of all time. "Coin by coin, set by set, you cannot beat this price," one of them exclaimed. As he and his confederate continued their repartee, they began to speculate how much certain coins in these sets would be worth if they were the numismatic equivalent of Bo Derek in the movie *10* "If you send that Kennedy half in and get it graded Proof 69—

$800," one of them fantasized. The reality, of course, is that after all these years, most of the Bo Dereks in 1960's proof sets have long since been discovered and someone else has pocketed the profit.

As always, however, the meat of the matter—after all the sizzle—was the price. The network was selling these 10 sets for $149.95, plus $9 postage and handling. And you could have beaten that price—beaten it to a pulp, in fact—at just about any coin shop or through mail-order ads in hobby periodicals such as *Coin World* and *Numismatic News*. One *Coin World* advertiser was offering these 10 sets at the time for an aggregate price of $92.85, plus postage and insurance, and he was charging only $4 for that.

The home-shopping hucksters are partial to Mint-packaged sets because the government holders lend greater credibility—almost an official imprimatur—to their offers. They also like to sell certified coins—coins that have been graded and encapsulated by the Professional Coin Grading Service, the Numismatic Guaranty Corporation of America and similar companies—because these coins are properly perceived as legitimate and liquid. Certified coins, however, represent good value only if they are sold at or below existing market levels. The TV salesmen price them well above those levels. To make matters worse, they misrepresent the market implications of grading-service data.

On one January 2002 segment, for instance, they touted the rarity of a "Year 2000 $50 Gold Eagle Perfect MS-70 NGC Certified" by reporting (presumably accurately) that only 201 examples of this coin had been certified as Mint State-70, the highest possible grade, by NGC. They failed to point out that many newly minted American Eagle gold bullion coins—for that is what this is, a one-ounce gold bullion coin—would merit that designation if they were submitted to NGC or any other grading service, for they are almost always well struck and lustrous and by their nature they see no use and tend to be preserved in that condition. Conceivably, NGC might end up certifying 2,001, 20,001—even 200,001—Year 2000 coins of this type as MS-70 if anyone thought it worthwhile to submit them. The number stood at just 201 at the time only because few had been sent in, not because few existed. There is little marketplace interest in high-grade examples of gold bullion coins; most people view them as hunks of precious metal, not collectibles. It might well be, in fact, that most (even all) of those 201 pieces had been sent to NGC by the TV shopping network specifically for use in this promotion. By the way, its asking price was $799.95, plus $9.60 shipping and handling. That's about three times what gold bullion was selling for at the time—and with all due respect to the coins' perfect grades, few collectors or dealers would have paid much more than the price of an ounce of gold.

Obviously, television time is expensive—even at 2:00 in the morning, when many of these coin segments seem to air. Likewise, it can be costly to place full-page ads in dozens of Sunday newspapers. Defenders of these practitioners cite this reality in an attempt to explain the relentlessly high prices they exact. Do these business costs, however, justify markups of more than 50 percent—often substantially more—over the prices for which the same items are readily available elsewhere?

Their defenders also argue that the TV shopping shows and Sunday-supplement ads are getting new people interested in coins and expanding the hobby's base. That may have been true to a limited extent with the 50-state Washington quarters, but most of the credit in that case belonged to the news media, which reported on the program extensively; the U.S. Mint, which advertised the coins widely in both print and electronic media, and the program itself, which provided something interesting and worthwhile for face value—a concept totally foreign to the Sunday-supplement and late-night shills.

▶ Avoiding Rip-Offs

There are a number of rules that will help you maximize the enjoyment you derive from your hobby and the value you receive in the coins you purchase. The caveats offered by Scott A. Travers, in his role as a consumer advocate, include the following:

- ▶ Deal with reputable dealers.
- ▶ Educate yourself, and buy the book before the coin.
- ▶ Be certain the dealer states *in writing* what grading standards are being used if you purchase coins that are not certified by grading services. Be sure, too, that you are paying a fair price for that standard—certified or otherwise.
- ▶ Use common sense, and look at the coins. If a coin is unattractive to you, no matter what anyone else says about it, don't buy it.
- ▶ Become familiar with the basic standards of grading services. Some services are strict; others are notoriously loose.
- ▶ Buy a rare coin, not just a certified product.
- ▶ Don't give your credit-card number to anyone that you haven't called.
- ▶ Take *immediate* action against anyone who has sold you overpriced or overgraded merchandise. Under the Uniform Commercial Code, you might have only four years from your date of purchase to take action. Government agencies such as the Federal Trade Commission have been very helpful in looking out for the public interest, but the FTC is structured in such a way that it helps consumers collectively, not individually.
- ▶ Save all original holders, receipts, canceled checks and other proofs of purchase.

Chapter 7

The United States Mint

"Uncle Sam, it is said, is the biggest coin dealer in the business." I wrote that in my weekly Numismatics column in *The New York Times* on June 8, 1980—and today, more than two decades later, those words are still right on the money. Besides producing far more coins for commerce than any other mint in the world, the United States Mint also sells far more collector coins and coin sets than any professional numismatist. Proof sets, "mint sets" and commemorative coins—all these and more are produced by the millions each and every year at Uncle Sam's mints and sold to the public at healthy markups. They earn a handsome return for the federal government. Unlike normal coin dealers, the U.S. Mint doesn't have to concern itself with maintaining a two-way market. One-way traffic is the rule: The Mint sells coins, but it never buys them.

This virtual monopoly comes with the territory. In drafting the United States Constitution, the Founding Fathers gave Congress the power "to coin Money, regulate the Value thereof, and of foreign Coin, and fix the Standard of Weights and Measures." Congress, in turn, established the U.S. Mint in 1792 to produce the nation's coinage according to a system set forth in the Mint Act that year—a decimal system whose cornerstone is the dollar.

The original Mint Act provided for 10 denominations: the copper cent and half cent; the silver dollar, half dollar, quarter dollar, dime and half dime (initially called the "disme" and "half disme"); and the gold eagle, half eagle and quarter eagle, with face values of $10, $5 and $2.50, respectively. Other denominations were added through the years, and the half dime eventually gave way to the base-metal copper-nickel five-cent piece we know today as the "nickel." Of those later additions, only the nickel remains in production today, along with half of the 10 original coins (all of which have undergone changes in size and composition along the way).

▶ The Early Years

The original Philadelphia Mint was the first building erected by the fledgling U.S. government. It came complete with an outbuilding used to stable horses—for horsepower, in the literal sense, played an important part in operating the Mint's machinery. The first U.S. coins were made with what are known as *screw presses.* The primary component of each of these presses was a massive iron screw with a coin die attached to a sleeve along its head. This die was aligned directly above a second die, and a planchet (or coin blank) was placed between them. Workmen then turned a weighted iron bar attached to the screw, driving the upper die into the planchet. This powerful blow simultaneously impressed the blank with designs from both dies. The resulting coin was then removed and a new blank was inserted.

Though primitive, this process was reasonably efficient: A skilled team of coiners could turn out several dozen smaller coins per minute. Agility was essential for the workman inserting planchets into a screw press—for if he mistimed his move, he could easily lose a finger. This risk was reduced at the Philadelphia Mint in 1793 when coiner Adam Eckfeldt invented a device that automatically fed planchets into the coining area and ejected the finished coins.

In 1816, the Mint began using steam power on a limited

The original Philadelphia Mint. The mint was built in 1792; this photo
dates from 1854, 21 years after it was replaced. *Photo courtesy R. W. Julian.*

basis—but not for striking coins. Screw presses continued to produce all U.S. coinage until 1836, when production was converted
to the new technology—one already being used widely in Europe.
With steam-driven presses, the Mint was able to increase its output
dramatically while, at the same time, turning out coins of superior
quality and greater uniformity. By the end of the 19th century, the

Street vendors outside the present Philadelphia Mint in 1976. Americans were celebrating the nation's Bicentennial at the time. *Photo by the author.*

A screw press. This was the type of equipment used to produce the earliest U.S. coins. *Illustration courtesy R. W. Julian.*

A steam-powered press. This equipment, used to produce U.S. coins from 1836 through the late 1800's, greatly improved the quality and uniformity of the coinage. *Illustration courtesy American Numismatic Association.*

Mint was using hydraulic presses powered by electricity, further enhancing its production capabilities in terms of both quantity and quality. One set of statistics illustrates tellingly just how far those capabilities—and the nation's coinage requirements—have come since the beginning: It took the Mint eight years, from 1792 to 1800, to produce its first million coins—and two centuries later, it could make a million coins in 20 minutes.

▶ High-Value Money

Making money is, of course, the U.S. Mint's first and foremost responsibility—making money, that is, in the sense of producing it. Making money in the sense of profiting from the process had a far more limited role in the Mint's early history. In fact, it wasn't until the mid-1960's that its profit margins really began to balloon.

The first U.S. coins had very high intrinsic worth: The value of the metal they contained was virtually the same as their stated value as money. The silver dollar, for instance, had a dollar's worth of silver, and the $10 gold piece was worth $10 just as a piece of gold. Even the pure copper cent and half cent provided very nearly a cent's or a half cent's worth of copper. This reflected the view of Alexander Hamilton, the nation's first Secretary of the Treasury, that making coins with less than a full measure of value would encourage counterfeiting. It also was meant to instill the public with confidence in the nation's money.

As time went by and the nation grew to maturity, there was less need to reassure the public by giving U.S. coins full intrinsic value. People had confidence in the federal government simply because of its size and strength. Nonetheless, the government continued to provide high metallic value in its gold and silver coins well into the 20th century.

▶ The Beginning of Debasement

Because of fluctuations in the value of gold and silver, early U.S. coins often came to be worth more as metal than as money. When this disparity grew sufficiently large, the undervalued coins were exported and melted by profiteers. At various points, Congress tinkered with the weight, size, fineness and composition of gold and silver coinage in an effort to discourage hoarding and melting and thereby ensure its continued circulation. But as late as 1850, nagging problems continued. The California Gold Rush was depressing the value of gold and, conversely, increasing the value of silver. U.S. silver coins soon reached and passed the critical point at which they could be profitably melted.

Faced with a serious shortage of silver coins, Congress took the first significant steps toward debasement of U.S. coinage. In 1851, it authorized the issuance of a silver three-cent piece with a fineness of only 75 percent, rather than the standard 90 percent. Then, in 1853, it trimmed the weight of the half dollar, quarter, dime and half dime by slightly more than 8 percent, thereby reducing their silver content by the same amount. For a three-year period, from 1853 through 1855, these coins bore arrows beside the date to denote their downsized status. The arrows were then removed, but the lower silver content was retained.

▶ Seigniorage

Though its primary motivation for that first modest debasement was to keep silver coins in circulation—a goal that it achieved—the change also brought a second important benefit to the Mint in the form of *seigniorage*. This word, of French derivation, literally means "something claimed or taken by a sovereign or other superior as his just right or due." In a coinage context, seigniorage is the amount by which the face value of a coin exceeds the government's costs in producing and distributing it. Profit earned by the Mint in this manner goes directly into the government's general fund.

There was little such profit in the Mint's first 60 years, since U.S. coins possessed such high intrinsic value. The 8-percent reduction in the silver coins' size translated into an 8-percent profit for Uncle Sam—and represented not only the first important debasement of U.S. coinage but also the first major enhancement of the U.S. Mint's seigniorage revenue. An even bigger step in that direction took place in 1857, when the pure copper "large cent" was replaced by a copper-nickel coin—the Flying Eagle cent—with less than half the weight and metal value. The half cent was discontinued at that time, thereby removing another unprofitable coin from the nation's coinage lineup and the Mint's balance sheet.

1857 Flying Eagle cent. The nation's first "small cent," this was an early step toward debasement of U.S. coinage. *Photos courtesy American Numismatic Association.*

Seven years later, the cent—by then bearing the Indian Head design—was reduced in weight by another one-third and its composition was changed from copper-nickel to bronze (copper, tin and zinc). In all, Uncle Sam slenderized the cent by 70 percent in less than a decade—and, in the process, he cut his production and distribution costs substantially.

Debased coins can be likened to *fiat money*—unbacked paper currency that can't be redeemed for coinage or precious metal of equivalent value. The Federal Reserve Notes issued by the Federal Reserve today are fiat money. The acceptance of such paper money—and of debased coinage—depends on trust in the government, rather than the value of the money itself.

▶ 'Clad' Coinage

From the 1850's onward, seigniorage was a source of significant profit, year in and year out, for the U.S. Mint. That profit skyrocketed, aptly enough, at almost exactly the time Uncle Sam began sending astronauts into space. In the early 1960's, the price of silver began to rise alarmingly and threatened to reach the point where—for the first time in more than a century—it would become profitable to melt U.S. silver coins for their metal content. The government couldn't stop people from hoarding (and eventually melting) existing U.S. coins, a process that already had begun and was exacerbating a nationwide coin shortage, but it could and did erect a firewall to ensure that future coins would not end up in melting pots. That firewall took the form of the Coinage Act of 1965.

Starting in 1965, dimes and quarters no longer would contain any silver. Instead, they would be made of two outer layers of a copper-nickel alloy bonded to a core of pure copper. The half dollar also would be a "clad" or "sandwich-type" coin, but it would retain a silver content of 40 percent—less than half the previous amount. (It, too, would become an entirely base-metal coin in 1971.) The new compositions were chosen partly because their appearance resembled that of silver and partly because their electromagnetic properties made them compatible with vending machines.

The hoarding of silver coins soon reached fever pitch, and those who saved large quantities put themselves in position to reap substantial profits—especially if they held them until the beginning of 1980, when silver soared in value to $50 an ounce. The biggest windfall, though, went to the U.S. Mint—and ultimately to the government's general fund. Whereas the Mint previously had realized a profit of about 10 percent on each silver coin it produced, with the remaining 90 percent representing its expenses, chiefly the cost of the metal, it now found those figures nearly reversed: With silverless "clad" coins, it was earning a profit of more than 80 percent in the form of seigniorage.

That profit has continued ever since, and it has been magnified by a huge increase in the Mint's production levels in the interven-

ing years. Prior to 1960, the annual output of Washington quarters, for instance, had exceeded 100 million only five times (all during the war years of 1941 through 1945). Since the advent of clad
coinage in 1965, it has frequently topped 1 billion. The Roosevelt
dime's mintage also has risen dramatically. Thus, the Mint has not
only been enjoying high seigniorage on each coin, but receiving
it on a vastly expanded volume.

The numbers are staggering: In Fiscal Year 1999, the Mint's
seigniorage profit totaled more than $1 billion. During that year,
Mint officials listed the cost of making coins at eight-tenths of a
cent apiece for the Lincoln cent, 2.6 cents for the Jefferson nickel,
2.1 cents for the Roosevelt dime, 3.0 cents for the Washington
quarter and 10.7 cents for the Kennedy half dollar. The Sacagawea dollar, introduced in 2000, could bring the government
enormous additional profit, for its cost is estimated at just 12
cents apiece. By the end of 2001, the Mint had made more than
a billion "golden dollars," representing seigniorage of close to $1
billion.

▶ Proof Sets and 'Mint Sets'

Seigniorage is the Mint's biggest money-maker, but it also has developed a secondary source of considerable income—and profit—in
recent years by producing and selling collectibles. Its most dependable sources of this profit are annual proof sets and uncirculated coin
sets (commonly called "mint sets" by collectors). The Mint has also
produced numerous commemorative coins since 1982, but its profits
from these have come largely in the form of the seigniorage they
have yielded. Although substantial surcharges generally are included
in the issue prices of these coins, this revenue normally goes to
organizations designated by Congress (typically beneficiaries associated with the subject being honored by the coins).

Proofs

Proofs are special coins made with the finest available materials and equipment—flawless coin blanks, highly polished dies and coining presses reserved for such production. The Mint strikes each proof more than once to give its design sharp detail, and the process also leaves the finished coin with impeccable surfaces. Most U.S. proof coins have brilliant, mirrorlike surfaces—and on early strikes from a given set of dies, the raised design elements may be frosted, a feature many collectors find very appealing. At various times in the past, the U.S. Mint also has made proofs with *matte* finishes, which have a sandblasted appearance.

1962 proof Washington quarter. Like most U.S. proof coins, this one has a mirrorlike finish. *Photos courtesy Scott A. Travers.*

Proofs were made occasionally in the Mint's early years—some as presentation pieces, others as an accommodation to collectors. As noted in Chapter 1, they were first offered to the public at large in 1858. Although sales increased in time, they remained relatively small until 1950, when the Mint resumed the production of proofs after an eight-year lapse and—for the first time—packaged them in complete sets. At that point, each set contained five coins— the cent, nickel, dime, quarter and half dollar—with a total face value of 91 cents, and the Mint sold and shipped them for $2.10 per set.

Buying proof sets from the Mint in the 1950's and early 1960's was like shooting fish in a barrel: Turning a profit was almost as certain for buyers as death and taxes. The sets could be resold for more than $2.10—often a lot more—the day they arrived in the mail. That would all change in the late 1960's. In 1968, after another lapse (this time three years), the Mint reintroduced proof sets with new packaging and a new price. The sets now came in hard plastic holders, rather than the flat, flexible Pliofilm sleeves in which they had been housed until 1964. And the issue price now was $5 per set—nearly two-and-a-half times the previous amount, even though two of the coins (the dime and quarter) no longer contained precious metal and a third (the half dollar) contained less than half as much as before.

The Mint had learned a lesson by watching collectors cash in their chips on earlier proof sets. From now on, it would share in the profits—or, as things turned out, make all the profits itself in many years. Even the new packaging, which the Mint cited as partial justification for the higher issue price, came to be viewed as a negative by collectors. Its bulky size greatly reduced the number of sets that could be stored in a safe or a safety deposit box—a problem that gave buyers an even more jaundiced view of these sets in years to come, when most of them remained persistent losers in the resale market.

Since 1968, the Mint has raised the issue price of proof sets numerous times—sometimes because it was adding a new coin or coins (the Eisenhower dollar in 1973, the statehood Washington quarters in 1999), and sometimes to cover other increased costs. By 1999, the issue price had reached $19.99. An encouraging move in the other direction took place in 2000, when the Mint actually added a coin—the Sacagawea dollar—without increasing the price of the set. Since 1992, the Mint has also issued annual silver proof sets, in which the half dollar, dime and quarter (five quarters per year during the 50 State Quarters Program) are 90-percent silver. As of 2001, these had an issue price of $31.95 per set. Yet another option, planned for the duration of the statehood quarter program, was a proof set containing just the five state quarters for each year, issued in base metal. As of 2001, the Mint was selling this set for $13.95.

Mint Sets

"Mint sets" provide uncirculated examples of all the U.S. coins produced for use in commerce during a given year. One coin is included from each mint that made it for circulation. Thus, the 2001 mint set has 20 coins—one sleeve containing the 2001 cent, nickel, dime, half dollar, Sacagawea dollar and all five 2001 state quarters from the Philadelphia Mint, the other sleeve containing the same 10 coins from the Denver Mint.

The Mint began issuing uncirculated coin sets in 1947. They have generally played second fiddle to proof sets because—unlike proofs—uncirculated coins can be obtained elsewhere at face value. In certain years, however, these sets have provided collectors with coins not available anywhere else. That happened, for example, in 1970, when the Kennedy half dollar was included in the mint set but never produced for circulation. It happened again in 1973 with the business-strike Eisenhower dollar from P and D mints. It also happened in 1981 with the Susan B. Anthony dollar from all three mints (Philadelphia, Denver and San Francisco). These mint-set-only coins have a modest premium value. As a rule, however, mint sets have sunk below their issue price in the resale market—primarily because the Mint has issued them at levels well above face value and they are, after all, just ordinary coins in mint condition. The 2001 mint set was issued at $14.95— nearly three times its total face value of $5.82.

▶ Commemorative Coins

As the name suggests, *commemoratives* are coins that commemorate—serve as a reminder of—some person, place or event, often on the occasion of a major anniversary The 50-state Washington quarters are commemorative coins, but unlike most such coins in the United States, they are *circulating* commemoratives—coins that are meant for use at face value in the nation's commerce. The Bicentennial dollar, half dollar and quarter of 1975–76 likewise were circulating commemoratives.

Most U.S. commemorative coins have not been intended for circulation. Rather, they have been low-mintage issues meant for sale at a premium to help raise revenue for some designated purpose. For example, the very first U.S. commemorative—the Columbian half dollar of 1892–93—was issued for sale at $1 each to help finance the World's Columbian Exposition in Chicago, a world's fair marking the 400th anniversary of Christopher Columbus' voyage of discovery to America. That coin, like all subsequent "commems," as collectors call them, required approval by Congress.

From 1892 through 1954, the U.S. Mint produced 60 different coins—48 half dollars, six gold dollars, two $2.50 gold pieces, two $50 gold pieces, one silver dollar and one quarter dollar—as part of what is now known as the "traditional" series of U.S. commemorative coinage. Among their more significant themes were the opening of the Panama Canal, the sesquicentennial (150th anniversary) of American independence and the 75th anniversary of the Civil War Battle of Gettysburg. Among their lesser subjects were the sesquicentennial of the city of Hudson, N.Y.; the tercentenary (300th anniversary) of York County, Maine; and the emergence of Cincinnati as a "musical center." The program reached full boil in the mid-1930's, when Congress was deluged with dozens of proposals and many reached fruition. It fell out of favor—with the Mint, with Congress and even with collectors—because of chronic abuses, including prolonged issuance of some commemoratives well beyond their intended year of issue (in one case over a period of 14 years), selection of themes that were parochial in nature and inequitable sales methods. In 1954, the U.S. Treasury put the whole program on hold—a hold that would last nearly 30 years.

Commemoratives got new life in 1981, when the Reagan Administration, in a move that caught collectors totally off guard, supported a proposal for a special half dollar honoring George Washington on the 250th anniversary of his birth. That 1982 silver half dollar ushered in the "modern" era of U.S. commemorative coinage. Attempts were made to avoid the abuses that had plagued the traditional era. For one thing, the coins were now being sold directly by the Mint, rather than under the auspices of local committees, as had been the case with the earlier issues. For another, they would be sold only in the authorized year of issue; in the past, local committees had been able to return for additional production if the authorized limit hadn't been reached in the first year.

Plaster model for 1982 George Washington commemorative half dollar. This was the first U.S. commemorative coin to be issued since 1954. *Photo courtesy James F. Lowney.*

Despite good intentions, modern commemoratives descended all too soon into abuses of their own. The U.S. Olympic Committee was a major accessory to these abuses, using its clout in Congress to secure the authorization of repeated coin programs—

even in years when the Olympic Games were taking place in other countries. In the first two decades of modern U.S. commemoratives, five different coin programs helped raise funds for Olympic-related causes. One of these, a 16-coin program for the 1996 Summer Games in Atlanta, was more than three times bigger than the largest previous program of U.S. commemorative coins (the five-coin 1915 set for the opening of the Panama Canal).

1988 Olympic commemorative silver dollar. One of numerous U.S. Olympic coins inappropriately issued in years when other nations were hosting the Games. *Photos courtesy United States Mint.*

Congress also cut itself in on the action, authorizing recurrent coinage programs heralding milestones in its own history and those of related institutions and raising millions of dollars for pet projects—among them improvements to the Capitol Building, the U.S. Botanic Gardens and the U.S. Capitol Visitors' Center.

Another problem with modern commemoratives has been issuance of coins for events of dubious significance. In 1991, for example, a silver dollar was issued on the 38th anniversary of the end of the Korean War—leading some wags to speculate that it must have been inspired by the 38th parallel, which separates North and South Korea. Another silver dollar marked the 10th anniversary of the Vietnam War Memorial in Washington—a little early for such a commemoration.

1991 Korean War commemorative silver dollar. Badly designed and dubiously timed, this coin marked the 38th anniversary of the end of the Korean War. *Photos courtesy United States Mint.*

Beyond these problems, the series also has suffered from wretched excess in the number of programs authorized and wretched artwork in many coins' designs. Some steps were taken to improve the situation in the late 1990's—in large part through the efforts of the Citizens Commemorative Coin Advisory Committee that had been brought into being in 1993 to help advise Congress on what could be done to remedy the proliferating abuses. By 2001, a limit had been established of two non-circulating commemorative coin programs per year. This was a flexible figure, but it had held fast for several years, bringing some semblance of sanity to the series.

▶ Mint Buyers, Beware

Buying collectible coins from Uncle Sam—proof sets, in particular—used to be a surefire way to turn a profit. That's no longer true. Now and then, a coin or coin set does increase in value, as happened in 2001 when the Mint sold 500,000 commemorative silver dollars with the same basic design as the old-time Buffalo nickel. Because of high demand and the modest mintage (relatively low by modern standards), these coins were soon selling for several times their issue price—even though that was inflated with a $10-per-coin surcharge. Far more often, the opposite has been true since 1968: The coins or sets sold by the Mint at a premium have fallen below their issue price—sometimes far below—and remained there.

One big reason is the law of supply and demand. As Scott A. Travers observes in his market-savvy book *How to Make Money in Coins Right Now, 2nd Edition* (House of Collectibles, 2001), "the coins being sold by the Mint are seldom truly rare; on the contrary, they are almost always struck in very significant numbers, well beyond the level that experienced collectors deem scarce, much less rare." Thus, even though there is decent initial demand for most Mint products, the supply almost always exceeds the demand in the resale market.

The lethal knockout punch for buyers' profit potential is the issue price level at which these coins and sets are typically sold. Despite the Mint's protestations to the contrary, proof sets—and even more so mint sets—have been overpriced since 1968 and the Mint has sought to camouflage this with fancy packaging. It would serve collectors' interests far better to dispense with the window dressing (which many find inconvenient anyway) and cut the price along with the packaging. At the very least, no-frills alternative packaging, sold at a lower issue price, should be offered.

In the case of commemorative coins, the problem takes the form of surcharges mandated by Congress. Typically, there is a $35 surcharge built into the issue price of a commemorative $5 gold piece and a $10 surcharge in the price of a silver dollar. These revenues normally go to the "worthy cause" that prevailed upon Congress to authorize the coins in the first place. Thus, collectors seeking such coins to maintain the completeness of their sets are forced to subsidize these causes—and, in the process, greatly diminish their prospects for future price equilibrium, much less gain.

The U.S. Mint consistently provides high technical quality in its collector coins (though the artwork often leaves much to be desired). For decades, however, it has given its customers generally low value and pocketed the lion's share of the profits.

Chapter 8

....

Errors and Varieties

....

Quality may be a dominant theme in the coin market today, but not all collectors are obsessed with finding the perfect coin. Some, in fact, spend much of their time looking for exactly the opposite—coins that are *imperfect,* to such an extent that they belong in a nickel-and-dime freak show. These dedicated hobbyists collect *mint errors,* and their numbers have increased dramatically in recent years, making error collecting one of the fastest-growing and most dynamic numismatic specialties.

Error coins are hardly a modern phenomenon; there have been minting mistakes since the dawn of minting itself. Indeed, they were far more prevalent in bygone days, when minting techniques were cruder and deviations from the norm were commonplace. Early U.S. coinage, for example, is replete with overdates—coins on which one or more of the numbers in the date were engraved over numbers from an earlier date. These would be considered first-magnitude errors if they occurred today, but they are so routine in coins from the early 1800's, particularly cents, that collectors treat them not as errors at all, but rather as die varieties. Part of the appeal of modern mint errors is the fact that major mistakes *are* relatively rare—that technical advances and quality control have reduced their occurrence to the point where they are merely a blip on the U.S. Mint's production radar screen.

Errors and *varieties* are closely related. In general, errors are coins that differ from the norm in ways unintended by the mint that produced them, while varieties are coins that differ from others of the same kind in ways that were planned by the mint. Thus, there are two *varieties* of the 1883 Liberty Head nickel because the U.S. Mint added the word "Cents" partway through production to clarify the value of the coin. Similarly, there are two varieties of the 1913 Buffalo nickel because the Mint modified the design after the start of production to reduce the coin's excessively high relief. These were not *errors* because the Mint meant them to be that way.

Errors, by contrast, tend to happen by accident; they're mistakes in the manufacturing process. Off-center coins result from misalignment of a die and the planchet during striking. Wrong-metal coins occur when an incorrect planchet is fed into the coining chamber. Broadstrike coins are produced when a planchet isn't held tightly by the collar during striking and the metal then spreads beyond the proper diameter. With overdate coins, it can be argued that there is an element of intent, since someone at the mint consciously chose to reuse old dies and engrave new numbers over old ones. That explains why the many early U.S. overdates are generally regarded as varieties, rather than errors; long-standing common usage has accorded them that status. In modern times, however, the U.S. Mint has officially frowned on such practices, so most collectors treat the handful of overdates from 1900 onward as mint errors. They are, in fact, among the most desirable and valuable of all U.S. mint errors.

▶ Modern Mint Errors

Some of the most dramatic U.S. mint errors of modern times have occurred while the nation was at war. This is no mere coincidence. Production requirements tend to expand in wartime while budget allocations shrink—a combination bound to put a strain on quality control. Moreover, key personnel may be summoned at such times to military service, placing the already heavier-than-usual burden in the hands of less experienced employees. So it was that in 1918, while American doughboys were fighting "over there" during the closing months of World War I, workmen pressed leftover 1917 dies into service to make small numbers of 1918 Buffalo nickels at the Denver Mint and Standing Liberty quarters in San Francisco. These 1918-over-1917 overdate coins, with the "8" engraved over the "7," are both extremely rare and highly coveted, and both are worth tens of thousands of dollars in mint condition.

A similar scenario unfolded in 1942, the first full year of U.S. military involvement in World War II—this time with the Winged Liberty (or "Mercury") dime. At both the main mint in Philadelphia and the Denver branch, small quantities of dimes were struck with 1941 dies on which a "2" had been engraved over the final "1." Actually, the engraving was so casual, even careless, that the "2" is almost next to the "1," rather than directly above it, so that the date appears to be 19412. Again, these proved to be major rarities and now command premiums ranging as high as five figures.

World War II witnessed another mint error that ranks today as undoubtedly the most famous ever made by Uncle Sam. In 1943, to conserve supplies of copper for urgent wartime needs, the U.S. Mint struck cents from zinc-coated steel. The experiment lasted for only one year, but it gave rise to an enduring rarity when handfuls of cents were struck at all three mints in the standard bronze alloy. These 1943 "copper pennies" have captured the public's imagination ever since, and even people totally oblivious to all other mint errors will almost surely be aware of these. They now routinely command strong five-figure premiums—sometimes even more. In the 2002 edition of his book *The Insider's Guide to U.S. Coin Values* (Dell, 2001), New York City coin dealer-author Scott

A. Travers listed the value of 1943 bronze cents at more than $100,000 in mint condition. He knew whereof he wrote, for in 2001 he had sold a Philadelphia Mint example of the coin, graded AU-58 by PCGS, for "about $100,000" to a West Coast collector. A more complete discussion of this intriguing rarity can be found in Chapter 12.

◗ The Growth of Error Collecting

Interest in mint errors got another boost in 1955, when some of that year's cents from the Philadelphia Mint turned up with obvious doubling of the date and the inscriptions on the obverse. These "doubled-die" cents weren't struck twice during the minting process; rather, they were struck with a die (or dies) on which the doubling already had been impressed. The error was easily discernible with the naked eye, and the coins caused quite a stir when they started showing up, primarily in the Northeast. It seemed at first, however, that they would be regarded chiefly as conversation pieces, rather than serious collectibles. Only with the passage of time did it become apparent that they had the appeal, and staying power, to become an important—and permanent—part of the mint-error pantheon. Today, mint-state examples bring thousands of dollars apiece, and circulated specimens sell for hundreds.

Another offbeat Lincoln cent—this time a variety, rather than an error—surfaced in 1960 and stimulated still more interest in numismatic oddities. Early that year, collectors noticed that the numbers in the date were significantly smaller on some 1960 cents than on others. They also observed that these "small-date" cents were considerably scarcer than their large-date counterparts—and that while they were produced at both the Philadelphia and Denver mints, those from Philadelphia were particularly

Closeup of date on 1955 doubled-die-obverse Lincoln cent. This dramatic mint mistake helped popularize error coin collecting. *Photo courtesy American Numismatic Association.*

scarce. Before long, rolls of small-date 1960-P cents were selling for about $400, or $8 per coin. It turned out that the Mint had enlarged the date early in the year, soon after the start of production, because the numbers were too small and were getting clogged.

The appearance of the 1955 doubled-die and 1960 small-date cents within such a short time planted the seeds for extensive growth in error and variety collecting. That growth was hastened by serious setbacks elsewhere in the hobby. First the bubble burst in the roll market, sending the prices of late-date coin rolls skidding and greatly curtailing activity in that area. Then, in 1965, Congress authorized removal of silver from the dime and quarter and reduction of the half dollar's precious-metal content—and soon this led to a drastic reduction in the number of desirable coins in circulation as old ones were hoarded and

Reverse of 1937-D "three-legged" Buffalo nickel. Excessive polishing of the die obliterated the bison's right foreleg, creating a valuable mint error. *Photo courtesy American Numismatic Association.*

Closeup of date on 1943-over-1942 Jefferson nickel. Mint errors are more common during wartime, when skilled workers are away and quality control is less stringent. *Photo courtesy One-Minute Coin Expert, from* Coin World.

seemingly worthless new ones flooded the nation. This one-two punch dealt a body blow to mainstream coin collecting, but, in the process, it sent determined hobbyists looking for new ways to collect—and many of them settled on error coins as a good alternative.

Error collecting became a growth area in more ways than one, for new "clad" coinage was made in such huge quantities—and with such headlong haste, at least in the beginning—that it spawned an unusually high volume of minting mistakes, some of them related to the cladding process itself and therefore never seen before in the United States. Some coins turned up, for instance, with one or both of the outer layers missing, so that the design was struck on the copper core. This bumper crop of errors provided a bonanza for the many new collectors pursuing this lively specialty. By the end of the 1960's they had formed their own national organization, Numismatic Error Collectors of America (NECA, for short), and were carving an important niche for themselves in the hobby.

▶ A Millennial Mother Lode

Error collecting enjoyed continued growth during the closing decades of the 20th century, boosted by periodic new discoveries that drew the attention of the media and the public and reinforced enthusiasts' resolve. Doubled-die cents appeared again, for example, in 1972 and 1995—and though neither was as obvious as the 1955, both were strong enough to stimulate interest and attract new collectors to the field. Now and then, coins turned up in proof sets without the "S" mint mark that all are supposed to have had since 1968. This occurred on small numbers of proof 1970 dimes, 1971 nickels and 1990 cents, and all of these—especially the cent—command impressive premiums.

2000 "mule" with (undated) obverse of state quarter and reverse of Sacagawea dollar. This coin changed hands for tens of thousands of dollars. *Photos courtesy "One-Minute Coin Expert."*

But none of this prepared collectors, or the U.S. Mint, for the dazzling array of spectacular new errors that burst upon the scene around the same time as the new millennium. Within a span of months in 2000, specialists were astounded by a series of discoveries so startling that some of them had no precedent in the Mint's more than 200-year history. Most stunning of all was a double-denomination "mule" bearing the obverse of a statehood Washington quarter and the reverse of a Sacagawea dollar. This coin, struck on a planchet meant for the "golden dollar," flew in the face of the long-standing belief that it would be impossible for the Mint to produce a coin mating two different denominations. The discovery coin, received from a bank by an Arkansas man, was sold in an auction soon afterward for just under $30,000. During the weeks that followed, half a dozen more examples turned up, and several changed hands for even higher prices.

"This coin is the modern or millennium edition of the 1804 silver dollar or the 1913 Liberty Head nickel," said Fred Weinberg of Encino, Calif., one of the nation's most prominent dealers in mint-error coins, likening the dollar/quarter mule to two of the most famous and most valuable of all U.S. coins.

Around the same time, the hobby was electrified by news of yet another double-denomination mule: a coin struck on a cent planchet with the obverse of a 1999 Lincoln cent and the reverse of a Roosevelt dime. The unimaginable—and supposedly impossible—now had happened twice in a matter of weeks or months.

Other incredible errors also began popping up:

- At least three 1999 Susan B. Anthony dollars struck on "golden" planchets meant for the Sacagawea dollar.
- A Maryland statehood quarter struck on a Sacagawea coin blank.
- A 1999 George Washington commemorative $5 gold piece struck on a dime planchet.
- A clad Washington quarter, thought to date from the mid- to late 1960's, certified as having two reverses and no obverse.

In its defense, the Mint pointed out that with the start of the statehood quarter program in 1999, it was producing record numbers of coins—28 billion in 2000 alone—and that the major errors made during that period represented a minuscule portion of its overall output. The high production level—24 hours a day, seven days a week for much of that period—undoubtedly accounted for many of the mistakes. However, something more sinister also was afoot: At the height of the excitement over the new errors, the Mint filed charges against a former employee at the Philadelphia Mint, charging him with stealing mint-error coins over a two-year period and selling them for a total of $80,000. The suspect denied producing the coins, claiming he simply smuggled out coins that he had come across in the normal course of his work.

Jay W. Johnson, who became Mint director in May 2000 and served until August 2001, is inclined to agree that most—if not all—of the error coins produced during that hectic period resulted from the strain on the mother mint's manpower and machinery, rather than a conspiracy to make such coins to order.

"It was a combination of factors," Johnson said in an interview conducted for this book. "Because of the heavy production demands, we weren't checking things as carefully as we should have been. We had a new production situation with the state quarters, and the old policies designed to catch such errors weren't being diligently followed. Also, we had a lot of new part-time employees who weren't that well trained and weren't being supervised as closely as they should have been, especially when they worked the second and third shifts."

When the errors began to turn up in greater than usual numbers and highly unusual forms, Johnson appointed a task force headed by himself to investigate what was happening and determine what could be done to stem the flow of errors from the mint. The group included key Mint production and security employees.

"The biggest thing we did," he said, "was enforce an existing policy that whenever the dies are changed, the first coins struck must be physically examined to make certain that nothing is wrong. If that had been done routinely, the mules would have been detected immediately and we would have corrected the problem before starting large-scale production. We did detect the errors, of course, and tried to destroy them before they got out, but a few of them managed to slip through.

"You have to be vigilant, and it takes everybody from the die person to the operator changing dies to the guy producing the coins and the counters and baggers. Everywhere along the line, we needed to be more vigilant."

1982-D Lincoln cent overstruck by a Roosevelt dime. Parts of the dime's design are clearly visible. *Photos courtesy Scott A. Travers.*

Johnson believes the arrested employee's story that he was removing coins already made, not creating error coins himself. As part of a plea agreement in which the employee admitted guilt, he gave Mint officials detailed information on how he was able to hide the coins and smuggle them out of the building. That was "extremely helpful," Johnson said, in enabling the Mint to take corrective measures and plug the security gaps that made the thefts possible. Beyond that, he said, the Mint's firm action in prosecuting the case served as a strong deterrent to other employees who might have been tempted to do something similar. The employee got a 10-year prison sentence. "We were very pleased with the sentence," Johnson said. "And we didn't have to post it on the bulletin board. Word of that traveled very quickly."

Roosevelt dime with a cud, or blob of metal, covering the date. A die break caused metal to flow into the damaged area, obliterating the date. *Photos courtesy Scott A. Travers.*

The Mint's corrective measures—regarding both security and production problems—evidently worked, for the number of major error coins entering circulation slowed to a trickle thereafter.

▶ State Quarter Errors

The state quarter/dollar mules and the Maryland quarter struck on a dollar planchet are aberrations unlikely to be encountered any more in circulation. Less dramatic—but nonetheless interesting— errors are relatively common, though, on statehood Washington quarters, and some of them can be worth hundreds or even thousands of dollars to their fortunate finders. Because the state quarters have such a broad base of collectors—and even non-collectors— pursuing them, errors that occur on these coins bring substantially higher premiums than similar mistakes on standard U.S. coins such as Jefferson nickels, Roosevelt dimes and older Washington quarters with the regular design.

Off-center Washington quarter from the 1980s. The dramatic degree of the off-center strike enhances the value of this coin. It would be worth even more if the date were fully visible. *Photos courtesy Scott A. Travers.*

Here are some of the errors you should look for—and might well find—among the statehood quarters (and other coins as well) in your pocket or purse:

▶ **Off-center coins.** If the planchet isn't properly aligned with the dies during striking, the resulting coin will lack the design in the area that was outside their range, and the visible portion of the design will appear off-center. This type of error is relatively common, especially on smaller coins; Lincoln cents just slightly off center may be worth no more than a dollar or two. By contrast, larger coins struck dramatically off center can be worth a great deal more, especially if the date is visible. A statehood quarter fitting this description might well be worth hundreds of dollars.

▶ **Clips.** These are coins with part of the metal missing, typically leaving a curved edge as if a metallic cookie cutter had sliced off part of the planchet. This type of error actually occurs during the stamping of planchets, not in the striking of the coins themselves. The value of such a mint error varies according to the size of the missing area and its location. Generally, coins with larger clips are more valuable, as are those on which the date and mint mark can be determined. At this writing in early 2002, statehood quarters exhibiting this type of error are worth from $20 to $100.

▶ **Clad coins with an outer layer missing.** The "sandwich-type" coins made by the U.S. Mint since 1965 have outer layers of copper-nickel alloy bonded to a core of pure copper. Occasionally, one or (rarely) both of these layers may peel off, leaving just the copper core to take the impression from the die. In the case of statehood quarters, the error is more valuable if it occurs on a coin's reverse—the side with the state design. The value can also fluctuate according to which state quarter is involved; the very first coin in the series—the 1999 quarter honoring Delaware—could easily bring a premium of $500 or more with this minting mistake. On other coins, the value would be less—perhaps $150 to $300.

▶ Closing Thoughts

Those who collect mint errors on more than a casual basis find themselves of necessity studying the minting process to learn how coins are made and how mistakes occur. This is one area where knowledge is definitely power—for the more a collector knows about the *normal* course of minting operations, the better equipped he or she is to recognize and evaluate deviations from the norm.

Overdates, off-metal coins and mules rank among the rarest and most valuable U.S. mint errors, with doubled-die coins also commanding big premiums on occasion. It is almost axiomatic that error coins increase in value as the errors become larger and more obvious. Errors are less common and more valuable on larger coins, because they are more likely to be spotted by mint inspectors and destroyed before they enter circulation. They also are more valuable if they appear on premodern coins—particularly those from 1836 onward, for that was the year when the U.S. Mint started striking coins with steam-powered presses and the quality and consistency of U.S. coinage improved enormously.

Chapter 9

....

The 50 State Quarters Program

....

Interest in U.S. coinage always gets a boost when something new and different comes along. That happened, for example, in 1964, when millions of Americans rushed to their local banks to get the newly minted Kennedy half dollar honoring the recently slain President John F. Kennedy. It happened again in 1975, when the U.S. Mint added special designs to three circulating coins—the Washington quarter, Kennedy half dollar and Eisenhower dollar— to mark the bicentennial, or 200th anniversary, of American independence. But nothing has ever stirred a greater groundswell of interest in the nation's pocket change and a higher degree of involvement—not only among collectors but also among the American public at large—than the 50 State Quarters Program.

"State quarters" first appeared in everyday circulation in January 1999, and almost at once they became the coveted objects of a nationwide treasure hunt. Their appeal was simple yet compelling: Each used the reverse of a regular 25-cent piece to showcase something special about one of the nation's 50 states. Thus, they not only gave Americans something new and intriguing to look for in daily commerce, but also provided a thumbnail history lesson— indeed, a whole *series* of lessons. Even their sequence contained historical insight, for the Mint was producing and distributing them in the order that the states joined the Union. In the case of the 13 original states, that meant the order in which the former colonies ratified the United States Constitution.

Reverse of 1999 Delaware quarter. This simple portrait of patriot Caesar Rodney racing to the Continental Congress got the statehood quarter series off to a fast start. *Digital image courtesy David L. Ganz.*

▶ **Delaware,** the first state to be featured, devoted its coinage "canvas" to a portrait of Caesar Rodney, a Colonial-era patriot, riding his horse from Dover to Philadelphia to cast a decisive vote in favor of declaring independence from Mother England.

▶ **New Jersey,** the third state in the series, borrowed the famous Emanuel Leutze portrait of Gen. George Washington leading his troops across the Delaware River on Christmas Day 1776 for a fateful surprise attack on unsuspecting Hessian soldiers the next day in Trenton.

▶ **Connecticut,** the fifth state, showed a stylized rendition of the old Charter Oak in Hartford, where local leaders hid the Colonial charter in 1687 to prevent its confiscation by an envoy of King James II.

Tens of millions of people began to look for the coins every time they got change at the supermarket, drugstore or bank—and as more and more of the quarters came out, appearing at the rate of one new coin every 10 weeks, they started assembling sets, housing their shiny treasures in boards or folders or maps obtained from local stores or in response to offers on TV. A survey commissioned by the Mint early in the program concluded that nearly one-half of all Americans—upwards of 120 million—were actively seeking out new statehood quarters and setting them aside. Far from waning, the level of interest seemed to be increasing as new coins continued to appear.

▶ The Origin of the Program

The Washington quarter is among the longest-lived of all U.S. coins, having been around since 1932—longer than any coin in the nation's history except the Lincoln cent. For most of that time, it attracted only modest interest from collectors. It was perceived as pedestrian in appearance, its mintages were relatively large, the series contained no major rarities and unlike Lincoln cents, which could be pulled from pocket change and set aside for just one cent apiece, saving Washington quarters required tying up 25 cents for every date-and-mint variety—a not inconsequential sum, especially during the series' early years, when "two bits" represented the cost of admission to a movie, or could have been used to buy two loaves of bread.

The coin fell even lower in hobbyists' esteem in 1965, when Uncle Sam stripped it of its precious-metal content. Up to then, it had been made from an alloy of 90 percent silver and 10 percent copper. From then onward, its composition consisted of two outer layers of copper-nickel alloy bonded to a core of pure copper. It was the coinage equivalent of fiat money: It had little intrinsic worth and its continued acceptance as a medium of exchange at its stated value of 25 cents depended entirely on public confidence in the government. Collectors—many of whom were treating the series already with a kind of benign neglect— now began to shun it altogether.

Given all these drawbacks, the Washington quarter was very much an ugly duckling—from a numismatic standpoint, at least—as the 20th century entered its final half decade. Events set in motion in 1995, however, would transform the coin before the century's close into a radiant swan. In the process, they would give the coin collecting hobby one of the greatest boosts it had ever enjoyed.

The 50 State Quarters Program bears a striking resemblance to a coin program carried out in 1992 by the Royal Canadian Mint. The similarity is more than coincidental, for Canada's program unquestionably served as a model—and, to some extent, an inspiration—for the American version. In 1992, Canada was celebrating the 125th anniversary of its confederation—the bonding of its individual provinces and territories into a single nation. To mark the occasion, it authorized the issuance of 12 special 25-cent pieces—one for each of the 10 provinces and two territories that made up the nation at the time (a new territory, Nunavut, was established in 1999). These "Canada 125" coins were issued at the rate of one per month during the anniversary year, with ceremonies heralding each new arrival. The program also included a single $1 coin to honor the nation as a whole.

Each of the Canadian 25-cent pieces bore a distinctive design on its reverse symbolizing some aspect of the province or territory being honored. (The standard coinage portrait of Britain's Queen Elizabeth II appeared on the obverse, or "heads" side, of each coin.) The series proved highly popular not only among Canadians but also among collectors in the United States. A number of American numismatists suggested at the time that a similar program ought to be considered by the U.S. Treasury and Mint. Prominent coin dealer Q. David Bowers, for example, proposed a series of special half dollars—commemorative in nature but issued for circulation—honoring the states of the Union. This, he pointed out, would cause minimal disruption because half dollars are little used in commerce—and yet would represent an inspiring, educational series of coins available to the public at face value.

◗ Key Players in the Process

One of the driving forces behind the 50 State Quarters Program was David L. Ganz, the managing partner of a New York City law firm, a coin collector since boyhood and, at the time he began to press the concept, the president of the American Numismatic Association. Ganz was named a charter member of the Citizens Commemorative Coin Advisory Committee in 1993, when that panel was established to advise the U.S. Mint on matters relating to commemorative coinage. He urged his colleagues to endorse the idea of circulating commemoratives—special coins with commemorative themes that were meant for circulation and issued to the public at face value, rather than being offered only as collectibles at a premium. At the time, Ganz was talking only in general terms; statehood coins hadn't yet been formally proposed. After considerable arm-twisting, he brought the committee—including its chairman, Mint Director Philip N. Diehl—around to his way of thinking. Diehl's support would be crucial in the subsequent maneuvering over the statehood quarter program, for many of the bureaucrats at the Mint, as well as the Treasury as a whole, were conditioned by years of official resistance to object reflexively to any proposed change in U.S. coin designs.

On July 12, 1995, the House of Representatives subcommittee on coinage held a hearing to consider the mounting concerns associated with U.S. commemorative coins—overproduction, overpricing and other nagging problems that had led to rising complaints and reduced sales. During that hearing, the congressmen heard testimony about Canada's successful 1992 coinage program and Harvey G. Stack, a longtime New York City coin dealer and prominent hobby leader, made a felicitious suggestion: Why not do something similar in the United States spotlighting the 13 original states?

The subcommittee chairman, Rep. Michael Castle of Delaware, liked the idea at once—especially when Ganz, also a witness that day, pointed out that Delaware would have the first coin in such a series, since it was the first state to ratify the U.S. Constitution. Following the hearing, Castle and John Lopez, his legislative aide, drafted a bill embodying the idea—but broadened it to include not just the first 13 states but all 50. Rather than proposing a series of special half dollars, as Q. David Bowers had suggested three years earlier, Castle called for quarters to carry the statehood designs—reasoning correctly that these would provide a more visible and meaningful form of tribute, since they circulate much more widely. His legislation specified that the coins should be issued at the rate of five per year for a period of 10 years—the timetable eventually adopted.

▶ The Rough Road to Passage

In retrospect, the merits of the statehood quarter program seem obvious. Besides creating enormous public interest in U.S. coinage and American history, it also has been a bonanza for the federal government, producing hundreds of millions of dollars a year in added *seigniorage*. As noted in Chapter 7, the U.S. Mint literally makes money by making money, since the face value of its coins exceeds their intrinsic worth and the other costs of producing and distributing them. At the time the state quarter program started, it was costing the Mint about three cents apiece to produce and distribute Washington quarters—giving it a profit of 22 cents each when they went on the books and entered circulation with a value of 25 cents apiece. Of course, it had been making a similar profit from previous Washington quarters, but the great interest in the state quarters—interest exceeding virtually everyone's expectations—led to the production of far more coins than usual and, in fact, far more than the already high projections. In 1998, the last year of the standard Washington quarter, the Mint produced slightly more than 1.7 billion quarters for circulation. In 1999, the first year of the state quarter program, total production jumped to more than 4.4 billion. That increase represented more than half a billion dollars in *additional* seigniorage. Production of statehood quarters rose sharply in 2000, approaching 6.5 billion, and comparable levels were anticipated during the remaining eight years of the decade-long program.

Given all this, one might assume that the state quarter program won quick and easy approval when the legislation came before Congress. On the contrary, it faced substantial resistance—primarily because of the deeply engrained suspicion of coinage redesign in the Treasury bureaucracy and, to a lesser extent, among some members of Congress and their staffs. Just a few years earlier, legislative proposals to update and upgrade the artwork on circulating U.S. coins had been beaten back by Illinois Congressman Frank Annunzio, then chairman of the House coinage subcommittee, in what appeared to be a personal vendetta against a leading advocate of coinage redesign. That left a residue of distaste for redesign in Congress. Meanwhile, career employees of the Treasury and the Mint had long been indoctrinated with the dubious belief, but official departmental view, that changing the designs on circulating coins would confuse the American public, lead to widespread hoarding and wreak unacceptable havoc in the marketplace.

These obstructions—and obstructionists—represented a formidable challenge for Congressman Castle when he introduced his statehood quarter bill, H.R. 3793, on July 11, 1996, almost exactly one year after the hearing where the concept first took root. A difficult struggle loomed, as David Ganz noted in his comprehensive book on the subject, *Official Guidebook to America's State Quarters* (House of Collectibles, New York, 2000). "The July 1995 hearing put the cart before the horse," Ganz wrote, "for even though the legislator was there, the rest of Congress and a recalcitrant bureaucracy had to be persuaded that the proposal made sense and was viable." By that time, Castle had developed a missionary zeal for the plan and he devoted unusual time and energy to rounding up support for it in Congress. In the meantime, Mint Director Diehl was waging a parallel battle against the "recalcitrant bureaucracy."

On Oct. 24, 1996, Congress passed legislation authorizing a new round of non-circulating commemorative coins—the kind made exclusively for sale at a premium as collectibles. As part of that measure, it called for a study of the statehood quarter proposal by Treasury Secretary Robert E. Rubin, but this was not an unalloyed victory for Castle, Diehl and other supporters of the plan. Their adversaries agreed to the study only because they believed that the Treasury would find the concept unfeasible. Indeed, many hobbyists held their collective breath right up to the time Secretary Rubin released his report on July 31, 1997—by coincidence, at a time when thousands of collectors were assembled in New York City for the annual convention of the ANA, the national coin club. Rubin expressed reservations—but gave a green light for the program to proceed. In essence, he didn't exactly endorse the proposal, but decided not to stand in its way. Months of intensive lobbying by Castle and Diehl had carried the day.

In all, it took three separate pieces of legislation to bring the program to fruition: the initial bill authorizing the study; the measure actually establishing the program—the 50 States Commemorative Coin Act—which was signed into law by President Bill Clinton on Dec. 1, 1997; and a follow-up bill, passed May 29, 1998, permitting rearrangement of statutory inscriptions on the Washington quarter. The last of these enabled the Mint to move two inscriptions—"United States of America" and "Quarter Dollar"—from the coin's reverse to its obverse in order to free more space for statehood designs on the reverse. To accommodate the added verbiage on the obverse, the Mint reduced the size of George Washington's portrait—the same basic portrait that has been on the 25-cent piece since 1932.

▶ Choosing the Designs

There was concern initially that some states, if left to their own devices, might choose designs that were undignified or otherwise inappropriate. One trial balloon, for example, suggested that the Illinois coin might feature Michael Jordan, then a high-profile basketball star for the Chicago Bulls. To keep the states from lurching into pop-culture designs, the legislation establishing the program was modified to include this clause: "No head and shoulders portrait or bust of any person, living or dead, and no portrait of a living person may be included in the design of any quarter dollar."

Under the legislation, design concepts originate with the states. They submit their ideas to the Treasury secretary and he passes them on to the Citizens Commemorative Coin Advisory Committee and the federal Commission of Fine Arts for comments and recommendations. The governor of each state then makes a choice. He or she is not bound by the panels' findings, but is expected to give them substantial weight. Generally, the governor's decision is implemented, but the Treasury secretary is the final arbiter and can amend—or even overrule—a state's design proposal.

Each state decides for itself how to obtain potential designs. Some states have set up Internet Web sites where residents could signify their preferences. Some have involved schoolchildren in the process; that was done, for instance, in Massachusetts, where the selected design—a Minuteman superimposed upon an outline map of the state—was a synthesis of proposals by two elementary school students. Some governors have appointed committees to come up with ideas and recommendations—as was the case in New Jersey, Ohio and Indiana, for example. Often, local artists have submitted designs—some of them quite elaborate: In Connecticut, art instructor Andy Jones furnished the striking interpretation of the Charter Oak that ended up being used on that state's coin. The results have varied widely in artistic merit. The Connecticut design is a superior work of coinage art, and some of the other designs also are aesthetically appealing. States that can take pride in their quarters' appearance include Connecticut, New York (the Statue of Liberty superimposed on an outline map of the state) and Rhode Island (a sailboat framed against a bridge in Narragansett Bay). At the other extreme, some of the designs are appallingly devoid of inspiration. The Pennsylvania and South Carolina coins, for instance, show cluttered compilations of state symbols, while New Hampshire's depiction of "The Old Man of the Mountain," a rock formation resembling a human figure, is all but undecipherable on such a small surface.

Reverse of 1999 Pennsylvania quarter. The second coin in the series ranks near the bottom aesthetically. Independence Hall, the Liberty Bell or both would have been better choices. *Digital image courtesy David L. Ganz.*

Looking back, the program undoubtedly would have benefited aesthetically from a more focused approach to obtaining designs, coordinated perhaps by a federally appointed panel of distinguished medallic artists and other knowledgeable individuals. Better yet, leading medallic artists might have been engaged to fashion the designs. This would have required the sacrifice of some of the state sovereignty and grass-roots participation by the public—both of which unquestionably have helped feed the program's popularity. The resulting artwork, however, would have made the series far more memorable and a source of much greater pride for the nation as a whole in years to come. Far from considering such an approach, the Mint appears to have gone out of its way to discourage and downplay involvement by professional artists. Even when a

2000 U.S. silver proof set. During the 10-year course of the statehood quarter program, the U.S. Mint is offering annual proof sets containing all five state quarters issued during each year. *Photo courtesy Scott A. Travers/United States Mint.*

statehood coin has carried a design by an identifiable artist, as in the case of Connecticut's Andy Jones, the Mint has withheld proper credit. More troubling yet, it has listed its own staff engravers as the designers in such instances—even though their role has simply been the technical task of converting the artists' work into coinable form (what is known as "executing" the designs).

▶ The Sequence of the Coins

The statehood quarters, like the states themselves, started in the East and then began moving westward. The Mint had finished striking coins for the 13 original states by the middle of 2001 and then made its way down the roster of the states that followed, one by one, as building blocks of the ever-expanding nation. As with the first 13 coins, the subsequent ones were scheduled for release in the order that each state joined the Union—starting with Vermont, which became the 14th state in 1791, and continuing all the way to Hawaii, the 50th state, which entered the Union in 1959. The Hawaii statehood quarter is to be the concluding coin in the series, making its appearance in October 2008. There are strong indications, however, that the series might be extended for one more year to permit the production of similar coins spotlighting the District of Columbia, Puerto Rico and four U.S. territories— Guam, the Virgin Islands, the Northern Marianas and American Samoa.

Double-struck state quarter obverse. The obverse (or "heads" side) is the same on all statehood quarters (though few have double heads like this one). *Photo courtesy Scott A. Travers.*

1999 New Jersey quarter with two clips. Individually, the clips are minor, but having two of them makes the coin more valuable. *Photo courtesy David L. Ganz.*

On each of the quarters, the name of the state appears at the top of the reverse, along with the year in which it attained statehood. The date at the bottom of the reverse is the year the coin was issued.

Following is the sequence in which the 50 statehood coins were scheduled to be released:

1999	2003	2007
1. Delaware	21. Illinois	41. Montana
2. Pennsylvania	22. Alabama	42. Washington
3. New Jersey	23. Maine	43. Idaho
4. Georgia	24. Missouri	44. Wyoming
5. Connecticut	25. Arkansas	45. Utah

2000	2004	2008
6. Massachusetts	26. Michigan	46. Oklahoma
7. Maryland	27. Florida	47. New Mexico
8. South Carolina	28. Texas	48. Arizona
9. New Hampshire	29. Iowa	49. Alaska
10. Virginia	30. Wisconsin	50. Hawaii

2001	2005
11. New York	31. California
12. North Carolina	32. Minnesota
13. Rhode Island	33. Oregon
14. Vermont	34. Kansas
15. Kentucky	35. West Virginia

2002	2006
16. Tennessee	36. Nevada
17. Ohio	37. Nebraska
18. Louisiana	38. Colorado
19. Indiana	39. North Dakota
20. Mississippi	40. South Dakota

▶ Premium Editions

Although the statehood quarters were conceived as circulating commemorative coins available at face value in ordinary pocket change, the Mint has also produced them in special collector versions meant to be sold to the public at a premium. Most of these are *proofs*—specimen-quality pieces struck multiple times on flawless planchets (coin blanks) with highly polished dies to impart both sharp detail and mirror-like, sometimes frosted surfaces. These are available as part of the annual proof sets produced by the Mint (which also include one example of each of the other current U.S. coins) or in separate sets containing just the five state quarters issued in a given year. The full proof sets can be obtained with either the standard copper-nickel quarters or with 90-percent-silver examples. Each silver proof set also contains a silver half dollar and dime.

Double-struck and clipped 1999 Connecticut quarter. Perhaps the most attractive state quarter, the Connecticut coin loses aesthetic appeal but gains considerable value because of a double mint error. *Photo courtesy David L. Ganz.*

Business-strike state quarters are included in the uncirculated coin sets (commonly known as "mint sets") which the Mint has issued during the course of the program. Each of these sets contains two examples of every coin issued for circulation by the Mint during that year—one from the main mint in Philadelphia and one from the Denver branch. The quality of the coins in these sets is generally superior to that of most other uncirculated coins made in the same year. But then, the sets carry a substantial surcharge over face value. In a sense, they represent a lazy approach to collecting state quarters. For most people, the appeal of these coins stems in large part from the challenge of tracking them down and the satisfaction of finding them.

Off-center 2000 Virginia quarter. Relatively common mint errors such as this are more valuable when they appear on state quarters because of the series' popularity. *Photo courtesy David L. Ganz.*

▶ The Future of State Quarters

Because they have such high mintages—levels exceeding 1 billion coins in many cases—the statehood quarters will never be mistaken for rarities. Pristine examples with very sharp strikes in very high grades are likely to enjoy premium value over the years, and in exceptional cases this could be quite substantial. The most valuable ones, and the ones with the greatest potential for future growth in value, are mint-error coins such as those discussed in Chapter 8. The popularity of state quarters should add to the appeal—and value—of these misstruck coins in future years.

Double-struck 2001 New York quarter. Miss Liberty carries two torches on this dramatic mint error. *Photo courtesy David L. Ganz.*

For the most part, the future appreciation of the 50 State Quarters is likely to come not in price, but in the satisfaction derived by those who put together sets of these fascinating coins. The dynamics of finding the coins, and filling the holes in folders, albums and maps, will change once all 50 quarters have entered circulation. In the early years of the program, people had the excitement of looking for each new coin as it made its debut. That recurring pleasure will be gone once the series is complete, but the sheer volume of coins dispersed in the nation's money supply will present a whole new challenge to enthusiasts.

The coins will serve as enduring reminders of America's history and heritage. And they will entice new generations of Americans, particularly young people, to learn more about the hobby that spawned this remarkable series.

···

Chapter 10

Bullion Coins

···

Decades have passed since precious-metal coins were last produced for commerce in the United States. The U.S. Mint hasn't struck silver coins for use in circulation since 1969 and hasn't made gold coins for that purpose since 1933. It does produce precious-metal coins annually, though, to be saved, rather than spent—and it has done so since 1986. They're called *American Eagles,* and they belong to a classification known as *bullion coins.*

Bullion coins are precious-metal coins whose value is determined at any given time by the "spot" price—that is, the current market price—of the bullion they contain. They are purchased and held as stores of value, not as collectibles, and their market value fluctuates in direct proportion to changes in the metal's intrinsic worth. This sets them apart from *numismatic coins,* whose value is determined to a substantial degree by the premium they command as collectibles. There can be some overlap. Numismatic coins made of gold or silver are worth at least as much as the metal they contain; it serves as a floor for their value in the coin market. To merit classification as numismatic items, however, they also must enjoy added value based on rarity, quality and other characteristics that stamp them as collectibles. Similarly, some coins minted specifically as bullion coins have come to be perceived as seminumismatic because they have low mintages or other features that make them appealing to collectors.

▶ A 'Mattress Mentality'

People who buy and hold bullion coins view them as a hedge against runaway inflation and other economic catastrophes. This is the kind of mentality that for centuries has prompted Europeans to hide gold under their mattresses for use in dire emergencies. Nor are Europeans the only ones who sleep with their security blankets under them, rather than over them. To cite just one high-profile example from recent history, Vietnamese refugees who fled to the United States following the fall of Saigon in 1975 did so on the strength of the gold—including gold coins—that they had socked away for such an eventuality.

Any precious metal or precious-metal coin can serve this purpose, of course, but gold has always been the tangible asset of choice. It packs its spending power in a form that is far more concentrated—and thus more portable—than silver. Although platinum may be more valuable than gold, ounce for ounce, at a given time, it's a far less flashy metal without the glitter and glamour that have led the human race to favor the gold standard from time immemorial. Thus, those who covet, acquire and hoard precious metal, including bullion coins, are characterized generically as *gold bugs*—even though their holdings may encompass other metals as well.

Americans who stuffed their mattresses—or socks—with gold in bullion form, including bullion coins, were doing so illegally prior to 1975. Under the Depression-era Gold Surrender Act, it was against the law to buy, sell or hold the yellow metal in that form. This was a double negative, and for once that didn't add up to a positive: It not only kept Americans on the sidelines in the market for bullion gold, but also held the market back from reaching its full potential. By the late 1960's, the price of gold had risen in world markets above the official level of $35 an ounce long observed by the U.S. government, and foreign investors were stashing it away in anticipation of further gains. Americans wanted a piece of the action, and pressure built in Congress to repeal the anachronistic sanctions on private gold ownership. The goldless society's guardians finally lost their fight to retain the status quo, and the ban was removed effective at midnight Dec. 31, 1974. To celebrate the occasion, The Franklin Mint struck a new 100-balboa gold coin for Panama just after the stroke of midnight.

The entry of Americans into the chase for gold bullion—and gold bullion coins—was expected to drive the prices of both sharply higher. Gold was already selling for close to $200 an ounce, and it was widely assumed that it would soar well above that level once Uncle Sam lifted his ban. Instead, the price *dropped* sharply on the day U.S. citizens regained the right to gold ownership and remained well below $200 an ounce for more than three years thereafter. Rather than jumping eagerly into this newly legal market, most Americans seemed to regard it with suspicion. By the end of the decade, however, they would shed their inhibitions and climb aboard the bandwagon—just as it began hurtling headlong toward a crash.

▶ The Great Bullion Boom

In the late 1970's, economic conditions worsened around the world. Trade deficits were taking a mounting toll on the U.S. dollar, and inflation was growing apace. The worse conditions got, the better the market became for precious metals. Gold opened 1978 at a 30-month high of $172.50 an ounce in London and moved up steadily from there. On July 18, 1979, it shattered the $300 barrier in London and less than three months later, on Sept. 29, it was selling for just over $400 an ounce in Hong Kong. The runaway bandwagon picked up speed in November

1979 when hostages were seized at the U.S. Embassy in Tehran, Iran, setting the stage for a 444-day standoff that added a new dimension to the nation's trauma—or "malaise," as it was called by President Jimmy Carter. As 1980 arrived, gold was selling for $634 an ounce and was headed much higher in a hurry. It reached an all-time high of $850 an ounce on Jan. 21, 1980—but then the bubble burst and the bandwagon crashed. The market went into a tailspin and in less than three months, on April 15, the price of gold slipped below $500 an ounce. It stabilized for a time, then began falling again, dropping below $400 an ounce on July 8, 1981.

Silver was taking a joyride of its own, with help from Texas oil tycoons Nelson Bunker Hunt and his brother Herbert, who sought to corner the market in the metal and nearly succeeded. In 1979, after several years in a fairly narrow trading range around $5 an ounce, silver began a meteoric rise paralleling that of gold. It set new records throughout the year in trading on the Comex in New York: $7.94 an ounce on Feb. 20, $11.02 on Sept. 4, $20.08 on Dec. 12. Finally, on Jan. 18, 1980, the Comex price soared to $50.35 an ounce—then suddenly collapsed. The Hunt brothers had overplayed their hand and overextended their assets—and in just four days, the price of silver plunged to $10.30 an ounce.

The great bullion boom coincided with a similar boom in rare coins. In truth, it was no coincidence; Coin dealers made tremendous profits during that period by purchasing gold and silver jewelry, silverware and other precious-metal objects from the public, then selling them immediately to refiners, and they used much of that money to buy rare coins. That, in turn, drove up coin prices to levels unimaginable prior to that time. Millions of Americans literally besieged coin shops in 1979 and the opening weeks of 1980 to sell precious-metal items—everything from wedding rings to gold teeth—and cash in on the big bullion prices. Coin dealers served as one of the principal conduits funneling such material to refiners.

▶ The Growth of Bullion Coins

At the time gold ownership was legalized for Americans, the dominant gold bullion coin was South Africa's *Krugerrand*. This 22-karat (.9167-fine) coin contains one ounce of gold and carries the portrait of Paul Kruger, the man for whom it is named, on its obverse. Its reverse depicts a springbok, a South African gazelle. Kruger, one of the nation's early political leaders, helped lay the groundwork for apartheid, South Africa's longtime policy of racial segregation. This connection— plus the policy itself —would contribute in time to the coin's demise.

One-ounce 1980 South African Krugerrand. This was the dominant gold bullion coin until it fell out of favor because of apartheid. *Photo courtesy South African Mint.*

At first, the main alternatives to the Krugerrand for Americans seeking bullion-related gold coinage were restrikes of such earlier coins as Austria's 100-corona and Mexico's 50-peso pieces, which contain slightly less than an ounce of gold and slightly more, respectively. The Krugerrand's popularity was due in no small measure to the fact that it provided exactly an ounce of gold, simplifying calculations of value. As the price of gold soared in 1979, Canada introduced a formidable new challenger known as the *Maple Leaf.* Like the Krugerrand, it furnished precisely an ounce of gold—but it did so in a fineness of .999, enhancing its appeal to gold purists. This coin bore the standard coinage effigy of Britain's Queen Elizabeth II on the obverse and a likeness of the maple leaf, Canada's national symbol, on the reverse.

From that point onward, action intensified in the bullion coin market—fueled not only by the increasing competition but also by the growing participation of American buyers, who had awakened to gold's possibilities during the dramatic run-up in bullion prices. In 1980, South Africa sought to attract less affluent buyers, plus gold jewelry users, by introducing Krugerrands in subsidiary sizes with one-half, one-quarter and one-tenth of an ounce of gold. Canada responded in 1982 with quarter-ounce and tenth-ounce Maple Leafs and a new front was opened in the "Great Bullion Battle."

Other countries joined the fray as the 1980's unfolded, but with far less impact than the Canadians. Some chose animal themes—China's Panda coinage, for example, and the Isle of Man's Cat. Britain made its bid in 1987 with the Britannia, which features a portrait of a graceful female figure personifying the nation. Some of the new coins achieved limited success but ended up filling niches, rather than enjoying broad-based sales. One of the less successful entries, and one of the more curious, was Australia's series of Nuggets—gold bullion coins depicting large nuggets discovered over the years, and even given nicknames, by prospectors Down Under. This series, introduced in 1986, petered out quickly as most bullion buyers chose not to get a piece of these particular rocks.

▶ The American Eagles

The United States stuck a timid toe into the gold bullion market-place in 1980, when it issued the first in a five-year series of "American Arts Gold Medallions." These were one-ounce and half-ounce gold pieces carrying the portraits of famous Americans who had achieved success in literature, music and other fine arts. Those chosen for this recognition included humorist Mark Twain, novelist Willa Cather and singer Marian Anderson. The "medallions" were intended to compete with the Krugerrand, but they never gained acceptance with gold bugs—largely because they were medals, not coins, and legal-tender status is a key considera-tion with many who buy such material. The U.S. Treasury sought to make them more coin-like in appearance in 1982 by receding their edges and adding beaded borders, but the effort came to naught and the program was abandoned after 1984.

American Arts gold medallions. Musician Louis Armstrong and architect Frank Lloyd Wright appeared on one-ounce and half-ounce U.S. gold pieces in 1982 as part of a four-year series. The "medallions" failed to win favor because they weren't coins. *Photos courtesy United States Mint.*

By 1985, anti-Krugerrand sentiment was building in Washington and calls were being heard increasingly for sanctions against the coin as a protest against South Africa's harsh racial policies. The "K-rand" was widely viewed as a symbol of apartheid, and 10 different bills were introduced in Congress in that year calling for curtailment of the coin's availability in the United States. On Oct. 1, 1985, President Ronald Reagan signed an executive order banning further importation of the Krugerrand—although he placed no curbs on the buying or selling of coins already being traded in the U.S. marketplace.

A vacuum had been created, and Congress moved quickly to fill it with new U.S. coinage—the American Eagles. The gold American Eagle was patterned closely after the Krugerrand in a deliberate bid to capture that coin's sizable market share. There were to be four coins—a one-ounce piece and fractional issues with gold contents of half an ounce, a quarter of an ounce and a

American Eagle gold bullion coins. Gold American Eagles, minted since 1986, come in four sizes—one-ounce, half-ounce, quarter-ounce and tenth-ounce. *Photos courtesy Scott A. Travers.*

tenth of an ounce   and their fineness was to be .9167 or 22-karat, just like the Krugerrand. The U.S. Mint sought to establish a link with traditional U.S. coinage by borrowing the obverse of the much-admired Saint-Gaudens double eagle ($20 gold piece) of 1907–1933 and placing it on the American Eagles' obverse. Inexplicably, it slenderized Miss Liberty in the process—which was roughly comparable to painting a mustache on the Mona Lisa. For the coins' reverse, the Mint chose a design by Houston artist Miley Busiek showing a family of eagles. The coins made their debut on Oct. 29, 1986 and quickly grabbed a healthy share of the market, accounting for sales of more than 2.3 million ounces of gold in their first six months.

In 1987, the Mint introduced a one-ounce silver American Eagle with a fineness of .9993. Again, the Mint went to its cupboard and pulled out a classic design—this time the obverse of the beautiful Walking Liberty half dollar of 1916–1947. That appears on the obverse of the silver American Eagle, while the reverse displays a heraldic eagle design by Mint staff engraver John Mercanti. A decade later, in 1997, the Mint began producing platinum American Eagles with the Statue of Liberty depicted on the obverse and an eagle in flight on the reverse. This comes in the same four sizes as its gold counterpart but is much purer, with a fineness of .9995

One-ounce silver American Eagle bullion coin. Photos courtesy Miller Magazines.

The U.S. Treasury sells American Eagles in large quantities to authorized buyers, who in turn sell them to major distributors. They filter down from there to individual dealers for retail sale to the public. The Treasury's initial charge reflects the spot price of the metal plus a small markup to cover the costs of production and distribution. Additional fees are imposed by distributors and dealers as the coins funnel down to the retail level. The premiums on the subsidiary gold and platinum coins are higher percentagewise than the markups on the one-ounce pieces because the production and distribution costs—which are constant—make up a greater proportion of the overall expense when applied to smaller amounts of precious metal. Likewise, the premium is significantly higher percentagewise on the silver coin than on the one-ounce gold and platinum Eagles because the costs, while similar, are being applied to a coin with much lower intrinsic worth.

All of the American Eagles are legal tender; they can be spent for face value and the U.S. government will redeem them upon demand for that amount. However, it's highly unlikely that any of the coins will show up in circulation, for their real value—and market price—at any given time is determined by the value of the metal they contain, and all bear denominations well below that amount. The one-ounce silver Eagle, for example, carries a face value of $1—but with silver bullion selling for roughly $4.50 an ounce in early 2002, dealers were selling the coin for $6.50 or more. During the same period, gold bullion was selling for about $280 an ounce and the one-ounce gold Eagle was bringing more than $300 at retail—yet its face value is only $50. The face values of the other three gold American Eagles are $25 for the half-ounce, $10 for the quarter-ounce and $5 for the ⅒-ounce piece. The platinum Eagles come in denominations of $100, $50, $25 and $10— and these again are well below their intrinsic worth, which has exceeded that of gold in recent years.

One-ounce Canadian Maple Leaf gold bullion coin. Canada also mints platinum Maple Leaf bullion coins with the same design. *Photo courtesy Scott A. Travers.*

▶ De facto Bullion Coins

Coins produced for use in circulation can serve as stores of value. However unlike American Eagles and other mint issues designated at the time of their manufacture as "bullion coins," these regular-issue coins were meant to be spent, not saved—at least at the time of their production.

One example of de facto bullion coins would be bags of common-date regular-issue U.S. silver coins in circulated condition. These are bought and sold routinely for just a nominal markup over their intrinsic worth as bullion—a markup that covers the seller's expenses in shipping and handling the coins, plus a modest profit. For all intents and purposes, these are bullion coins. To illustrate the point, one advertiser in a January 2002 issue of *Coin World,* a weekly hobby newspaper, was offering bags of 90-percent-silver U.S. dimes, quarters and half dollars—each with a face value of $1,000—for $3,495 delivered, based on a silver price of $4.40 an ounce. Each bag contained approximately 715 ounces of silver, "give or take a little because of wear on the coins." The price represented a surcharge of $349 per bag over the bullion value of $3,146—and according to the advertiser, this was about $200 over their "meltdown value," meaning that shipping and handling cost $149 per bag. That's a premium of about 6.35 percent over the coins' bullion value, which compares favorably with the markup on silver American Eagles.

For a somewhat higher markup, about 15 percent over bullion as of January 2002, a buyer can obtain a bag of common-date U.S. silver coins in mint condition. That modest differential in premium could prove to be money well spent, for the higher grade level gives the coins potential added value as collectibles. Many so-called "common-date" silver coins were consigned to melting pots at the height of the bullion market boom in 1979 and 1980, and some of the survivors could turn out to be scarcer than people realize.

Common-date regular-issue U.S. gold coins offer similar opportunities—although, because of their much higher intrinsic worth, they are typically traded in small quantities, often single coins, instead of rolls or bags. When the gold bullion market is quiet, as it was for the most part from 1985 through 2001, common-date Saint-Gaudens double eagles, in particular, tend to trade for only a nominal premium over their bullion value in grade levels of Mint State-60 and below—and even in somewhat higher mint-state grades, they can be obtained for relatively reasonable prices.

"The price of average uncirculated Saint-Gaudens twenties has been amazingly cheap in the last few years," said Steve Blum, a New Jersey coin dealer who bought and sold large quantities of bullion and numismatic gold coins while operating a coin shop in Manhattan for many years. "At certain times, there's really no premium on them. They represent an excellent deal—but unfortunately, there aren't as many places to buy them as there would be to buy American Eagles or Maple Leafs."

One-ounce British Britannia proof gold bullion coin. Introduced in 1987, this is among the most beautiful bullion coins. *Photos courtesy British Royal Mint.*

▌ Collectible Bullion Coins

In theory, bullion coins are intended for investors, not collectors. They are sold on the basis of their precious-metal value, not for their rarity or quality. In practice, however, some bullion coins have been marketed as collectibles. All of the American Eagles, for example, are struck by the U.S. Mint each year in proof editions that are sold for issue prices well above their bullion value, then change hands in the resale market for premiums as well in many instances. These premiums are based partly on the coins' superior quality and partly on their generally low mintages.

One-ounce Australian Nugget gold bullion coin. One of the least attractive bullion coins. *Photos courtesy Scott A. Travers.*

China's Panda coinage is another example of "numismatic bullion"—or at least the Chinese government has been striving to make it so by limiting mintages and varying designs every year. Even without the variety of playful, endearing images, the basic design benefits from the worldwide popularity of the native Chinese animals for which the coins are named. The very first one-ounce gold Panda, issued in 1982, had an unusually low mintage of 15,871 and rose in value within five years to nearly $1,400—or about three times the value of an ounce of gold bullion at the time. In 2002, two decades after its issuance, that coin was selling for only about $500—almost twice the much-reduced value of its bullion but far less than it had brought in the late 1980's. It still possessed appeal as a collectible, but its bullion aspect had suffered from reduced demand for gold.

One-ounce Chinese Panda gold bullion coin. Some consider the Panda partly numismatic because of its low mintages and attractive designs. *Photos courtesy Scott A. Travers.*

As a general rule, it makes more sense to purchase a numismatic coin at a bullion-related price than to pay a numismatic premium for a bullion coin. One is a collectible by nature, whose value is reinforced by its precious-metal content. The other is a piece of precious metal staking a possibly dubious claim to add-on value as a collectible.

....

Chapter 11

Coin Collecting
and the Internet

....

Coin collecting has changed with the times—and never more so than in the modern era, when it has grown explosively to accommodate the many new enthusiasts who, unlike their forebears, have found themselves with both time and money for such pursuits. It literally moved from the drawing room to the living room in the early part of the 20th century—and as the 21st century dawned, it was spilling over into the kitchen in millions of American homes as families gathered to fill the holes in coin boards with statehood Washington quarters.

The start of the new millennium came hard on the heels of another historic beginning: the start of the "computer revolution." As the 20th century ended, personal computers were getting to be as common in homes throughout the nation as microwave ovens, videotape recorders and electric toothbrushes. As millions of Americans became computer-literate and surfed the "information superhighway," coin collecting began to adapt to this development, too. Hobbyists found ways to meet, converse and correspond with other collectors on the Internet, to tap important sources of online information; and to buy and sell coins electronically. This learning process still was evolving as the new millennium started, as was the related technology. Up to that point, the marriage of coins and computers had been a mixed blessing—opening doors to new opportunities but also creating trap doors for the unwary.

▶ Buying and Selling Coins Online

The Internet's greatest impact on numismatics has been its rapid development as a venue for buying and selling coins. Its market niche was minimal in the early 1990's, but barely a decade later it made up a major sector of the marketplace, with annual sales totaling many millions of dollars. Its potential seems unlimited, for technological breakthroughs are making it ever easier for consumers—including collectors—to transact business online. As this is being written in early 2002, one of the largest computer manufacturers has just introduced, at nominal cost, a computer that fits in a user's pocket yet provides as much power and memory as standard desktop computers from just a few years earlier. This handheld computer can access the Internet from remote locations, making it possible to purchase coins from online Web sites or participate in online coin auctions—and examine photographs of the coins on the screen—white relaxing on the beach at a tropical resort.

In time, computer technology undoubtedly will reach the point where collectors can not only view photographs of coins online but actually see and manipulate three-dimensional likenesses of the coins—tilting and rotating these and looking at them from different angles, as they would do with the coins themselves, to determine their grade. A photograph, no matter how good, is really just a two-dimensional picture, so that would be a major step toward making online coin sales even more "virtual." The computer world is changing—and changing the world of coins—before our very eyes, and endless possibilities loom just over the horizon.

Online coin transactions take place in three primary ways—on Internet coin exchanges, through direct sales and in Internet auctions. Each of these has positive features but also downsides.

▶ Internet Coin Exchanges

Online coin exchanges are primarily the province of dealers, rather than collectors. However, they provide a good opportunity for collectors to look over dealers' shoulders, so to speak, and get a sense of what coins are worth in the marketplace. As this is written, the dominant exchange is the Certified Coin Exchange (or CCE, for short). Using their computers, member dealers post sight-unseen bid and ask prices on the CCE for certified coins in various series and grades. They can do so for coins from any of four different grading services—PCGS, NGC, ANACS and ICG. Those who wish to do so can execute trades at any time at the posted prices.

For a nominal fee, consumers can monitor the action on the CCE and view the transactions being consummated there by experienced dealers. This can be not only an interesting "spectator sport," but also a source of valuable information on the current state and possible future direction of the marketplace. It's much more expensive to register as a trader on the exchange, making this practical only for full-time dealers. For details on how to monitor the exchange, go to its Web site at www.certifiedcoinexchange.com and follow the instructions posted there.

▶ Direct Sales

Coins can be purchased directly from sellers at numerous online Web sites, and many of these sites are maintained by highly reputable dealers—including some of the nation's biggest and best professional numismatists. The problem is, some of the other sites are maintained by unscrupulous profiteers, and ordering coins from them could be the beginning of a painful and costly lesson in online economics.

The Internet is an untamed frontier. Online sales have grown at such a phenomenal rate that federal regulators haven't yet caught up with them. As a result, "merchants" with larceny in their hearts can and do victimize the unwary by misrepresenting their goods, shipping inferior products—and sometimes simply shipping nothing at all. In time, they may be tracked down and penalized for their misdeeds—but that may be too little, too late to help you recover the money you laid out to buy their inferior (or even invisible) wares.

When purchasing coins—or anything else—on the Internet, buyers need to exercise the same caution and prudence they would bring to similar purchases offline in their everyday pursuits. Before doing business with an online coin dealer, they should first determine whether he or she is a member of the American Numismatic Association (ANA), the Professional Numismatists Guild (PNG) or other leading hobby organizations. That type of involvement would indicate that the seller has standing in the hobby and isn't just a fly-by-night predator.

Buying coins online is quick and easy; instead of sending a check to a mail-order dealer and waiting a week or more, possibly even several weeks, for the check to clear and the coins you've ordered to be sent, you simply furnish your credit-card number and—presto!—the coins are on their way. It's up to you, however, to spend some time *before* placing your order checking out the background of the dealers to whom you're entrusting that all-important number. You also should make certain, when buying coins by credit card online, that the browser you are using is encrypted at 128 bits. If it isn't, your personal information could be stolen and you could become a victim of identity theft.

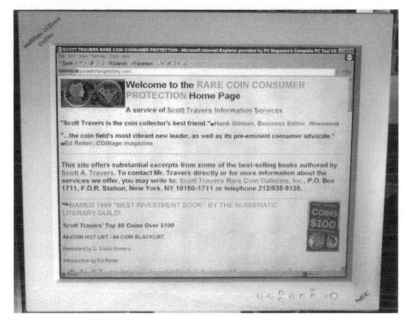

A coin dealer's Internet Web site. Online coin sales and informational serv-ices have increased dramatically in recent years. *Photo courtesy Scott A. Travers.*

▶ Internet Auctions

There are several major types of Internet coin auctions. In one type, the company conducting the sale has physical possession of the items being sold but doesn't own them; instead, it serves as a sort of clearing house for consignments placed by the coins' actual owners. Teletrade is perhaps the best known firm doing business in this manner. It has been doing so since 1986, and it has an exemplary track record for shipping coins to the winning bidders upon an auction's conclusion. A second type of auction involves buying coins through a bidding competition at a dealer's Web site. As in the case of buying coins directly from an individual dealer, this type of auction requires the exercise of caution, since the value you receive will be only as good as the ethics of the auctioneer you are dealing with.

The third major type of online auction—and the most popular—involves the use of a "facilitator site" provided by a company such as eBay. Unlike Teletrade, eBay doesn't have possession of the coins (and other merchandise) being sold on its Internet site. The coins remain in the hands of their consignors, who might be around the corner from you or halfway across the world—or, in some cases, might be nowhere at all, at least in terms of having any coins or honest intentions. With sellers in this last category, you might end up nowhere, too, in terms of getting anything back for your money.

Companies such as eBay are simply conduits. They provide the Internet "auction rooms" where dealers conduct sales, but they distance themselves from any responsibility for what takes place in that room. At the same time, they create the impression through their advertising that they are directly involved in these operations, and that gives bidders a false sense of confidence. Buyers reason that this large online auction firm will safeguard their interests and protect them from fraud and misrepresentation—when, in reality, they are at the mercy of the person or company actually selling the coins or other merchandise.

Scott A. Travers, a New York City coin dealer, author and consumer advocate, has had a number of consumers bring eBay-related problems to his attention.

"Not a week has gone by recently," Travers reports, "when I didn't have complaints from people who have had bad experiences buying coins at eBay auctions. The problem with eBay is, it wants to have it both ways. It wants to take credit for being a reputable site where you can do all your shopping with ease and with security. At the same time, it washes its hands of any fraud or deceit that occurs on its site."

In Travers' view, Internet coin buyers bear a good deal of responsibility for steering clear of such problems in the first place. "When you think about it," he says, "the easiest way to avoid these abuses isn't to criticize eBay, but rather to get consumers to deal with only reputable sellers. Virtually every dispute that I have seen on eBay could have been prevented if the consumer had just used common sense and taken proper precautions, such as buying coins graded by *reputable* grading services and dealing with dealers who are members of the ANA and PNG."

▶ The U.S. Mint Online

The United States Mint has established a major presence on the Internet. Since launching its Web site in April 1999, the Mint has built it steadily into a highly visible source of information on new collector coins and a very busy venue for sales of those products. Proof sets, mint sets, commemorative coins and statehood Washington quarters all can be purchased online from the Mint—and the rapid growth of sales volume indicates that more and more collectors and other consumers are placing their orders in this manner now, rather than by mail, fax or phone.

Preliminary figures indicated that the Mint sold more than $125 million worth of coin-related merchandise over the Internet in 2001, and sales appeared likely to be substantially higher in 2002. The Mint prefers to do business this way because it is more efficient and less expensive—and it has been giving incentive to would-be buyers by making online transactions cheaper for them, as well. Customers who order by phone or fax are charged a shipping and handling fee of $3.95 per order, but the fee is not applied to online orders.

The U.S. Mint Web site—www.usmint.gov—is more than just an online store. Among other things, it also offers games, cartoons and quizzes on coin-related matters for younger collectors; copies of the Mint's latest press releases; and historical information on the Mint and U.S. coinage through the years. Its primary function, however, is to showcase the various products the Mint is selling, and to give the public an easy way to purchase those items through a few computer keystrokes.

▌ Useful Web Sites

The author and publisher do not monitor the text or images contained on Web sites. Information is provided here solely as a convenience to Web users.

Clubs and Organizations

American Israel Numismatic Association
www.amerisrael.com

American Numismatic Association
www.money.org

American Numismatic Society
www.amnumsoc.org

British Art Medal Society
www.bams.org.uk

British Royal Mint
www.royalmint.com/

Canadian Numismatic Association
www.canadian-numismatic.org/

Canadian Numismatic Research Society
www.nunetcan.net/cnrs.htm

Classical and Medieval Numismatic Society

www.nunetcan.net/cmns.htm

Gold Institute

www.goldinstitute.com

International Bank Note Society

www.public.coe.edu/~sfeller/IBNSJ

John Reich Collectors Society

www.logan.com/jrcs

Numismatic Bibliomania Society

www.coinbooks.org

Numismatic Literary Guild

www.numismaticliteraryguild.org

Professional Numismatists Guild

www.pngdealers.com

Society for U.S. Commemorative Coins

www.money.org/clubs/suscc.html

Society of U.S. Pattern Collectors

www.uspatterns.com

Token & Medal Society

www.money.org/clubs/tams/index.html

USENET Newsgroup

news:rec.collecting.coins

U.S. Mint

www.usmint.gov

U.S. National Numismatic Collection/Smithsonian Institution

www.americanhistory.si.edu/csr/cadnnc.htm

Periodicals

Canadian Coin News

www.canadiancoinnews.com/

Celator, The

www.celator.com

COINage magazine

www.coinagemag.com

Coin Dealer Newsletter, The

www.greysheet.com

Coins Magazine

www.krause.com/coins/cm

Coin World

www.coinworld.com

Numismatic News

www.krause.com/coins/nn

World Coin News

www.krause.com/coins/wc

Commercial

Bowers & Merena Galleries Inc.
www.bowersandmerena.com

Certified Coin Exchange
www.certifiedcoinexchange.com/

Coin Facts.com Inc.
www.coinfacts.com

David Hall Rare Coins
www.davidhall.com

David L. Ganz
www.americasstatequarters.com

eBay
www.ebay.com

Heritage Capital Corp.
www.heritagecoin.com

Ira & Larry Goldberg Coins & Collectibles Inc.
www.goldbergcoins.com

National Gold Exchange
www.ngegold.com

Numismatic Guaranty Corporation of America Inc.
www.ngccoin.com

Professional Coin Grading Service

www.pcgs.com

Scott Travers Rare Coin Galleries Inc.

www.pocketchangelottery.com

Stack's Rare Coins

www.stacks.com

Superior Galleries

www.superiorgalleries.com

Teletrade

www.teletrade.com

....

Chapter 12

Ten Great Coins

....

Every coin has a story to tell. Some are more interesting or significant than others, but every coin—no matter how humble or inconsequential it may seem—is a bookmark in the annals of human history, and once we turn to that page we find ourselves immersed in an often engrossing tale. Romance, intrigue, mystery and conflict—all of the elements that make up mankind's experience are mirrored in coinage down through the ages.

U.S. coinage abounds with all these elements, and thousands of stories could be mined from this rich mother lode. In this chapter, we close our *New York Times Guide to Coin Collecting* by taking a closer look at 10 of the more fascinating numismatic nuggets.

▶ The Indian Head Cent

It's hard to imagine a time when the omnipresent Lincoln cent wasn't an integral part of American commerce—and American culture. The coin has been around since 1909, a claim that can be made by no other current U.S. coin and few of the people who use it. At one time, however, the now-hoary Lincoln cent was the new coin on the block, and the coin that it replaced was the one that conveyed the impression of having been around since the nation's birth.

That coin was the Indian Head cent—and while it didn't date

1860 Indian Head cent. The Indian cent was copper-nickel from 1859 to 1864, when its composition was changed to bronze. *Photos courtesy Scott A. Travers.*

back to the Continental Congress, its origins did predate the Civil War, and its 50-year life span was considerably longer than that of most other U.S. coins. It was longer, in fact, than the life expectancy of the average American at the time.

When people see a "penny" lying on the ground today, they often walk right past it; the coin is widely regarded as next to worthless. Things were far different in the mid-1800's. In those days, the cent was a coin of consequence, and with good reason: Ten cents an hour was considered a living wage, and the cent possessed substantial buying power. By the 1850's, however, the large copper cent being minted at the time had become—quite literally—too big for Americans' britches. The coin was almost as bulky as today's half dollar, and after a while carrying cents around could easily wear a hole in a person's pocket.

The U.S. Mint conducted a series of experiments with other coinage metals and smaller sizes—even preparing pattern coins, made of debased silver, with large holes in the center (a device intended to reduce the amount of metal without any sacrifice in diameter). At first, the Mint strove to keep the coin's intrinsic value high, believing that without such metal value, a new cent would be rejected by the public. As time went by, however, Mint Director James Ross Snowden came to the conclusion that unlike higher-denomination coins made of gold and silver, minor coins—including cents—enjoyed acceptance primarily because they were U.S. government issues, and didn't need metal value to reinforce this. This change in philosophy gave the Mint more options, and by 1856 it had settled upon a much smaller cent made from an alloy of 88 percent copper and 12 percent nickel. The obverse of this coin portrayed an eagle in flight, causing it to be dubbed the Flying Eagle cent.

The small cent—equal in diameter to today's Lincoln cent but nearly twice as heavy—was an instant hit with the public. Mint Director Snowden, however, wasn't completely satisfied. For one thing, the new coin wasn't striking up very well; high points on one side didn't always coincide with low points on the other, and this—combined with the hardness of the nickel in the alloy—led to many weakly struck pieces. Snowden also felt the design could be improved. The Mint's chief sculptor-engraver James Barton Longacre fashioned more than a dozen prospective new designs— many of them refinements of the Flying Eagle version, which also was his creation.

At length, the chief engraver came up with a portrait of a girl— ostensibly an Indian, but more likely a Caucasian—wearing a feathered headdress. This design was chosen to replace the flying eagle with the start of cent production in 1859. The new reverse featured a simple laurel wreath around the words "One Cent." A charming story has it that Longacre's daughter Sarah posed for the "Indian" portrait, but there's no apparent basis in fact for this seemingly apocryphal tale.

Americans have loved the Indian Head cent since the day it first appeared, and it rivals the Buffalo nickel—and even the Lincoln cent—as the U.S. coin with the greatest sentimental appeal. "Great art the coin was not," Cornelius Vermeule wrote in his classic book *Numismatic Art in America,* "but it was one of the first products of the United States mints to achieve the common touch and to identify itself with the transitions from frontier to industrial to social expansion during its decades of circulation, from 1860 to 1930."

Copper-nickel Indian Head cents—commonly known as "white cents" because of their light tan color—were minted each year from 1859 through 1864, reaching a total output of more than 150 million. Few of these circulated widely at the time, for Americans were hoarding all U.S. coins—even lowly cents—during the darkest days of the Civil War. In the absence of government coinage, merchants and promoters began to issue cent-sized bronze tokens, which came to be known as "Civil War tokens." These gained wide acceptance as a money substitute—and in 1864, they led the Mint to redo the cent along similar lines. From then through the end of the series in 1909, the Indian cent was bronze and 50 percent lighter in weight than the original.

Bronze Indian cents remained in production without interruption for nearly half a century, including the years when real-life Indians were fighting most fiercely to preserve their tribal lands from being overrun by American settlers. By the time the series ended, the West had been won and all but two of the lower 48 states had joined the Union. Throughout this long series, mintages of the coin were remarkably consistent. Production exceeded 100 million just once, in 1907, and dipped below 1 million only twice. By contrast, Lincoln cents routinely are made by the billions every year. The 1909-S, one of only two Indian Head cents minted in San Francisco, has by far the lowest mintage: At 309,000, it's scarcer than even the 1909-S VDB Lincoln. But the 1877, with a mintage of 852,500, is considerably more valuable because far fewer examples were set aside.

Although the series is lengthy in chronological terms, a complete set (not counting major varieties) encompasses only 54 pieces because there are just two branch-mint issues (the 1908 and 1909 cents from San Francisco); all the rest were minted in Philadelphia. It's a set that can be completed in circulated condition without taking out a second mortgage, but those who insist on choice mint-state specimens can count on spending tens of thousands of dollars.

▶ The 1943 Bronze Lincoln Cent

Most rare coins mean little or nothing to the average man or woman in the street. Ask most people about the 1794 silver dollar

1943 bronze Lincoln cent. Standard Lincoln cents issued in 1943 were made of zinc-coated steel. *Photo courtesy Scott A. Travers.*

or the 1894-S Barber dime or the 1916 Standing Liberty quarter and you might as well be discussing the average nighttime temperature on Mars. The "copper" Lincoln cent of 1943 is a different story. Millions of Americans have heard about this coin—even though they may not have the slightest interest in coin collecting otherwise. It isn't the most valuable U.S. coin ever made, but it may well be the most famous from the standpoint of the non-collecting public.

Officially at least, the United States Mint never has acknowledged that bronze cents were made in 1943. The cent's composition had been altered that year to conserve supplies of copper, which were needed for military purposes during that crucial stage of World War II. Instead of bronze (an alloy of copper, zinc and tin), 1943 cents were made of zinc-coated steel. When new, the coins had a shiny gray appearance not unappealing to the eye—but merchants complained that they looked too much like dimes, causing expensive confusion. What's more, they had a tendency to turn unsightly and rusty in circulation. With the wartime economy humming and demand for coinage high, the Mint cranked out a total of more than a billion cents that year—the lion's share being made at the nation's mother mint in Philadelphia. It abandoned the experiment the following year, however, making cents in 1944—and the next two years, as well—from the brass in GIs' salvaged cartridge cases.

Despite official denials, reports began to circulate almost immediately that some "copper pennies" had been minted in 1943. It's unclear whether these resulted from actual discoveries or rumor-mongering—but the latter seems more likely, since the earliest reported appearance of such a coin at a public auction didn't take place until 1958. The coin was withdrawn from that sale, reportedly because of insufficient interest—a curious development, considering the attention these coins have always attracted over the years. It may be that bidders were fearful that the coin would be seized by the Secret Service as an illegal issue. That didn't happen, convincing many observers that the government wouldn't challenge private ownership of such cents.

Apparently, those who owned these coins were not completely satisfied that they would be safe from confiscation, for little or nothing was heard of any changing hands for more than 20 years. Then, in 1981, Bowers and Ruddy Galleries of Los Angeles offered one for sale—an "extremely fine" specimen—at an auction held in New Orleans, and the coin brought $10,000. That was an auction record for any mint-error coin up to that time. Since then, public sales have become more frequent and prices have risen sharply. In 1999, a '43 bronze cent certified as Mint State-61 sold for $112,500, and several others also have realized prices in the $100,000 range in recent years. Almost all of the genuine specimens identified so far have been circulated coins, suggesting that the coins escaped detection initially despite the speculation about their existence.

John J. Ford Jr., a respected numismatic researcher, has estimated that 20 to 30 bronze cents were issued inadvertently during 1943—most of them at the Philadelphia Mint. That figure corresponds closely to the number that have been certified and encapsulated by coin-grading services. Examples from all three mints have been discovered, but as of this writing just one has been found from the Denver branch.

Ford offered a plausible explanation for how the bronze cents came to be made. "In the early 1940s," he noted, "the planchet-feeding mechanism for one-cent pieces consisted of galvanized chutes with straps. Presumably, some of the bronze planchets got hung up in the straps in December 1942, when production for that year ended. Then, when the steel blanks came along early in 1943, they pushed the bronze pieces along and they, too, were struck by the presses. Because of the war, the Mint had trouble getting competent help. So the quality control was not as good as usual at the time. A lot of copper cents were caught, I assume—but others got by and proceeded to enter circulation."

In much the same way that bronze cents were produced in 1943, a minuscule number of steel cents came to be made and released the following year. The 1944 steel cents are believed to be just about as scarce as the 1943 bronzes, but they never have enjoyed the same degree of publicity. Although they command significant premiums when they come up for sale, these tend to be considerably lower than those of the '43 bronzes.

Over the years, fast-buck artists have copper-plated 1943 steel cents and offered them for sale as genuine—and supposedly highly valuable—1943 "coppers." They also have altered the date of 1948 cents, which are bronze, to make the "8" look like a "3." Copper-plated "steelies" are easy to detect: A magnet will pick them up, while genuine bronze cents won't be attracted. Altered-date cents of 1948 are easily recognizable upon close examination of the "3."

Scott A. Travers, a New York City coin dealer, author and consumer advocate, has been an active bidder on bronze 1943 cents, buying one for a client at a 2001 auction for a price in the neighborhood of $100,000. He showcased that coin in a consumer report on NBC News and it generated thousands of responses. "Everybody knows about 1943 copper pennies," Travers concluded.

Another leading coin dealer, Q. David Bowers of Wolfeboro, N.H., had a similar observation. "The '43 copper cent is a very romantic piece," Bowers remarked. "It's a coin that appeals to the man in the street, and that enhances its aura and its value."

▶ The Two-Cent Piece

In the short term, the two-cent piece was a coin of no great consequence. It was minted for just 10 years, in quantities that dwindled annually—and in its final year, it wasn't even made for circulation, being produced exclusively in a proof version meant for collectors. Its long-range significance has been tremendous, though, for this was the coin that introduced the motto "In God We Trust."

1864 two-cent piece. This short-lived coin was the first to carry the motto "In God We Trust." *Photos courtesy Krause Publications.*

God is never dead in times of war. That was apparent all over again in the wake of the terrorist attacks of Sept. 11, 2001, when "God Bless America" became a national hymn, just as it had been in the depths of World War II. War bestirs soldiers—and nations— to seek hope and solace in the bosom of religion. So it was in the early 1860's, when the bloody Civil War sent Americans searching for consolation and guidance from above.

A second search was under way at the U.S. Treasury in 1863— a quest for coinage that people would spend, not save. By the beginning of that year, virtually all U.S. government coinage had vanished from circulation as frightened Americans hoarded it compulsively. An even more devastating crisis was averted when resourceful entrepreneurs devised an ingenious replacement: They issued bronze tokens that carried an implied—or even explicit—promise of redemption in goods, services or money. These "Civil War tokens" enjoyed broad acceptance and served for the duration as a useful (though inadequate) money substitute.

In most cases, Civil War tokens had the same diameter as the Indian Head cents then being minted by the government. They were thinner, though—and rather than being made of a copper-nickel alloy like the Indian cents of the day, they were bronze. By using cheaper metal and smaller amounts, the merchants who issued the tokens were able to achieve a greater profit—and because bronze is more malleable, production was easier.

It had long been assumed that Americans would reject debased coinage—coins whose face value greatly exceeded the value of the metal they contained. The initial success of the small-size cent upon its introduction in 1857 had suggested that the populace was willing to accept a tradeoff in the case of the "penny," giving up full value in return for greater convenience. Only after seeing the bronze tokens' liquidity did government officials fully grasp how far money-starved Americans would go. Mint Director James Pollock noted this in his annual report of Oct. 1, 1863.

"Whilst people expect a full value in their gold and silver coins," Pollock wrote, "they merely want the inferior money for convenience in making exact payments and not at all for the value of the copper, tin or nickel which may be present." He went on to propose that the cent's metal content be modified so that it "shall be composed of 95 per cent copper; remainder, tin and zinc in suitable proportions."

Three months later, Pollock sent a letter to Treasury Secretary Salmon P. Chase in which he urged not only a metallic makeover for the cent but also the authorization of a new coin—a two-cent coin—of the same bronze composition. He reasoned that thinner cents made of bronze, modeled after the popular Civil War tokens, would help overcome the coin shortage through the sheer volume that could be pumped into circulation—especially when paired with a two-cent piece doing double the work. Events soon proved him right: Following their issuance in 1864, the new coins won ready acceptance and reestablished a presence for federal coinage, effectively supplanting the substitute money.

The mating of the two-cent piece with the motto "In God We Trust" appears to have been a marriage of convenience. Secretary Chase had been pondering the placement of some such inscription on one or more U.S. coins since early in the war, and the two-cent piece—because it was brand new—made this possible without undue disruption. Up to then, U.S. coinage had never made mention of a supreme being, but the strong religious fervor born of the Civil War created a climate conducive to the use of such a motto. Historians credit a Baptist minister, the Rev. Mark R. Watkinson of Ridleyville, Pa., with planting the seed that led to this unprecedented action. In a letter to Chase in 1861, Watkinson had urged that provision be made for "the recognition of the Almighty God in some form on our coins."

"This," he said, "would relieve us from the ignominy of heathenism. This would place us openly under the Divine protection we have personally claimed."

The seed evidently took root, for as discussions proceeded on a possible two-cent piece, Chase made a point of calling for the placement of some such motto on the coin. The exact wording "In God We Trust" didn't come from Watkinson; rather, it evolved as the coin-design process moved along. Initially, Mint Chief Engraver James Barton Longacre fashioned two pattern two-cent pieces bearing not only dissimilar designs but also different inscriptions. One of the patterns featured a right-facing portrait of George Washington on the obverse, with the words "God and Our Country" above the bust. The other—which was adopted—depicted a simple shield with crossed arrows running through it; above this, a scroll proclaimed,

"God Our Trust." On both patterns, and on the coin itself, the reverse was dominated by the statement of value "2 Cents" within a wreath of wheat, encircled by the words "United States of America."

Over the years, the motto "In God We Trust" was added progressively to other U.S. coins as well. It has appeared on every denomination since 1938, when the Buffalo nickel, the last coin lacking this inscription, gave way to the Jefferson version—which ironically honors a man viewed by some as an atheist. The motto's use wasn't mandated until 1908—and even then, the order applied only to gold and silver coins. It wasn't until 1955 that Congress enacted legislation requiring the inscription on all U.S. coins and paper money.

▶ The 1913 Liberty Head Nickel

It is clearly illegitimate—and it might have been ruled illegal as well at one time. However, the 1913 Liberty Head nickel has risen above its disreputable beginnings to become one of the most famous—and most valuable—of all United States coins. It ranks today as the numismatic equivalent of a rock superstar or a matinee idol. In 1996, it became the first U.S. coin to exceed a million dollars at public auction—and when it comes up for sale now, the question is no longer whether it will sell for more than a million dollars, but how many millions it will bring.

1913 Liberty Head nickel. Only five examples are known to have been made. *Photos courtesy American Numismatic Association.*

The U.S. Mint never has acknowledged the existence of this coin. Officially, the Liberty nickel series—distinguished by a large "V" (the Roman numeral for "5") on its reverse—ended in 1912, closing out a 30-year run. As far as the Mint is concerned, the only five-cent piece produced in 1913 and bearing that date was the newly introduced Buffalo nickel, but ample opportunity existed for chicanery—and it seems abundantly clear that someone at the Mint answered that knock when it came.

The Mint had prepared dies for a 1913 Liberty Head nickel, just in case the Buffalo design—for whatever reason—had to be abandoned. The dies were locked in a vault at the Philadelphia Mint, along with those for the new Buffalo coin, and should have been destroyed once the latter went into production. Instead, at least five examples—all of them proofs—were struck with the Liberty Head dies.

The coins didn't surface for seven years; collectors had no hint of their existence, in fact, until an unusual ad appeared in *The Numismatist*, the official monthly journal of the American Numismatic Association, in December 1919. The ad, placed by one Samuel W. Brown of North Tonawanda, N.Y., offered to pay "$500 cash" for any 1913 Liberty Head nickel—"in Proof condition, if possible." Shortly thereafter, Brown disclosed that he had purchased five such coins and sold them all, for $600 each, to Philadelphia dealer August Wagner.

Reaction to all this turned from skepticism to surprise—and finally to cynicism—as the facts began to unfold. The most fascinating fact concerned the employment history of Samuel Brown, the man whose supposed hunch concerning the Liberty nickels proved to be so profitably correct: It turned out that Brown was a former Mint employee. What's more, he had worked at the Philadelphia Mint from 1903 to 1913, and was thought to have had access to the dies for the 1913 nickels. Although it has never been proven in a court of law, or acknowledged by those involved, it is generally believed that Brown himself struck the coins—or had them made by an accomplice—and then held them secretly after leaving the Mint in order to avoid suspicion. By intriguing coincidence, 1920—the year when he announced their "discovery"—also marked the end of the seven-year statute of limitations for prosecuting anyone who might have removed the coins illegally in 1913.

The dealer who purchased the coins promptly resold all five of them to Col. Edward H. R. Green, son of Hetty Green, the eccentric financier known as the "Witch of Wall Street" who was said to be the world's richest woman. Green held all five until his death in 1938, after which his holdings were dispersed. Over the years, the 1913 nickels grew steadily in both stature and value. Many doubted their legitimacy, but no one could question their rarity. If anything, the mystery surrounding their origin only served to enhance their mystique and appeal.

Beyond their rarity, the coins had the advantage of continuing publicity—generated largely by B. Max Mehl of Fort Worth, Texas, one of the nation's largest and best-known coin dealers from the 1930's through the mid-1950's. Mehl made them famous—and gained tremendous exposure for himself, as well—by placing nationwide ads offering to pay $50 each for any and all specimens he was offered. He knew that none would turn up (aside from the original five, which were of course tightly held and worth a great deal more than $50)—but most Americans didn't, and so they searched their pocket change, hoping to find a small fortune. The process produced converts for the hobby, customers for Mehl and new renown for the 1913 nickels.

A second old-time dealer, J. V. McDermott of Milwaukee, played a key supporting role by giving people a chance to see the rare nickel at close range. McDermott had purchased one of the five examples in Colonel Green's collection when the set was broken up, paying the princely sum of $900—and during the 25 years he owned the coin, it was on exhibit almost constantly. He displayed it at coin events all around the country, and thereby gave the nickel and its story vivid meaning for thousands of collectors—and non-collectors, too. Aubrey E. Bebee, a prominent dealer from Omaha, Neb., bought the McDermott specimen in 1967 for $46,000—a record price for any coin at that point. Bebee and his wife, Adeline, later donated the nickel to the ANA Museum in Colorado Springs, Colo.

In May 1996, the 1913 nickel from the world-renowned collection of Louis E. Eliasberg Sr. came up for sale at a New York City auction and was hammered down for $1,350,000. A 10-percent buyer's fee brought the bottom line to $1,485,000—the highest price ever paid for any U.S. coin up to that time and the first to break the million-dollar barrier. The record was short-lived; the 1804 silver dollar from the same collection broke it the following year, and yet another 1804 dollar raised the bar much higher—to $4,140,000—at a 1999 auction, also in New York and also conducted by the same company, Bowers and Merena of Wolfeboro, N.H. The 1913 nickel, however, will always have the distinction of membership number one in the Million Dollar Club of rare coins. This million-dollar baby truly has come a long way.

▶ The Buffalo Nickel

It isn't the most spectacular U.S. coin. It isn't the most dazzling. The Buffalo nickel can lay claim, however, to an even more signif-

1937-D Buffalo nickel. This famous five-cent piece is widely considered the most truly American of all U.S. coins. *Photos courtesy Scott A. Travers.*

icant superlative: It is the most distinctly American coin ever issued by Uncle Sam. Indeed, the two symbols that dominate its design even have "American" in their names: The obverse portrays a Native American, while the reverse depicts an American bison.

Some of the greatest U.S. coin designs were inspired by foreign models. The Saint-Gaudens double eagle was patterned, for example, on the coinage of ancient Greece, while the Walking Liberty half dollar Americanized "The Sower," a classic female figure on earlier French coinage. The Buffalo nickel, by contrast, is a genuine American original. Its inspiration came from America's Western frontier, and it has now become a part of the Old West's legacy itself.

The Buffalo nickel evokes nostalgia for the days when Indian tribes and bison roamed the range. Those days had been filled with hardships and hazards for white settlers migrating westward, but that starker, grimmer side was fading into memory at the time the coin debuted in 1913. By the turn of the 20th century, the tribes had been vanquished and confined to reservations and the bison had been slaughtered to the point of near-extinction.

The notion of using these symbols on a coin came from James Earle Fraser, a distinguished sculptor known for his realistic Western-themed works. In 1910, Fraser had learned that federal officials were considering redesign of the five-cent piece, which had borne the old-fashioned Liberty Head portrait since 1883. He expressed interest in submitting prospective designs and was encouraged to do so. The subject matter wasn't preordained; the Treasury's objective was simply to update the coin, in line with the improvements that already had been made with the introduction of new gold coins in 1907 and 1908 and the launch of the Lincoln cent in 1909. Fraser pondered other possible subjects, but soon turned to the theme he knew best—Western Americana.

"My first objective," he later explained, "was to produce a coin which was truly American, and that could not be confused with the currency of any other country. I made sure, therefore, to use none of the attributes that other nations had used in the past. And, in my search for symbols, I found no motif within the boundaries of the United States so distinctive as the American buffalo."

The Buffalo nickel didn't break new ground in depicting a Native American. "Indian head" portraits already had appeared on several other U.S. coins—notably the Indian Head cent of 1859–1909. Most of those earlier "Indians," however, were imposters: Caucasian models were used in preparing the designs, and then headdresses were added. Fraser did exactly the opposite, using Native American models and dispensing with the fancy headdress.

Over the years, there has been much speculation regarding the identity of the Indian chief portrayed on the famous nickel. Fraser reportedly said that he used several different models and blended their features into a composite portrait. The models are believed to have included a Sioux chief named Iron Tail who fought against Custer at Little Big Horn; a Cheyenne chief named Two Moons; and an Iroquois chief named John Big Tree. The bison on the coin's reverse was modeled after Black Diamond, a superb animal then on public view at the New York Zoological Gardens. In 1915, just two years after being immortalized on the nickel, this magnificent creature was callously sold and slaughtered when it reached the age of 20.

Although it is a masterpiece of naturalistic art, the Buffalo nickel was flawed from a technical standpoint: Its relief was unusually high, making the highest points prone to excessive wear in circulation. The very first strikes in 1913 showed the bison on a mound, but the Mint changed this at once when that portion of the coin evidenced a tendency to wear. The urgency stemmed from the fact that the mound served as the location for the statement of value, and Mint officials feared that the vital words "Five Cents" would wear away. Partway through production that year, the base was changed to a straight line, with the statement of value recessed below the line. As a result, 1913 nickels come in two distinct varieties, which collectors refer to as Type I and Type II.

One of the most famous and fascinating Buffalo nickels is the so-called "three-legged" mint error struck at the Denver Mint in 1937. It's theorized that a workman polished one of the dies after it became clogged during production and, in the process, he rubbed away the bison's right foreleg. On three-legged nickels, only the right hoof remains. There's no way of telling how many of these error coins were made, but the number is thought to be small and this is reflected in their price: In mint condition, the coin costs thousands of dollars, and even in lower grades it sells for hundreds.

Those are fancy prices, but they pale by comparison with the value of another mint-error Buffalo nickel made at the same mint nearly two decades earlier. In 1918, small numbers of nickels were struck in Denver with a 1917 die on which an "8" was engraved over the "7." This was apparently an economy move made to cut down on production costs during that wartime year. Over the years, collectors have made far more money from this 1918-over-1917 overdate coin than the government saved at the time. Today, mint-state examples bring tens of thousands of dollars.

The Buffalo nickel was minted for only 25 years—the minimum period specified by law. It was retired in 1938 to make way for Thomas Jefferson and his Virginia homestead, Monticello. The public loved the coin, but by then a move was afoot to turn U.S. coinage into a portrait gallery for great presidents, and Jefferson had been chosen to join Abraham Lincoln and George Washington, who were already featured on the cent and quarter, respectively. The Buffalo nickel continued to circulate until the 1960's and has long been among collectors' special favorites.

▶ The Kennedy Half Dollar

Where have all the half dollars gone? The question is seldom asked, for Americans have grown accustomed to the absence of this once integral cog in the nation's money supply. It's a valid one, however, and the explanation lies in a curious amalgam of miscalculation, poor timing and plain bad luck.

1964 proof Kennedy half dollar. This enormously popular coin hastened the demise of half dollars in general as circulating coins. *Photos courtesy David L. Ganz.*

To a great extent, the death of the 50-cent piece as a circulating coin resulted from the birth of the single most popular coin ever issued in this denomination—the Kennedy half dollar. Americans literally loved this coin to death when it made its first appearance in 1964, hoarding it in such quantities that it never established a presence in circulation. Although the U.S. Mint has continued to produce it in the intervening years, it has never regained a foothold in commerce for this formerly essential denomination.

This is more than a little ironic, for the Kennedy coin itself was brought into being by the death of the man it portrays. Seeking appropriate ways to honor John F. Kennedy in the chaotic days following his assassination on Nov. 22, 1963, federal officials decided that a coin would be a fitting and lasting tribute. There was precedent for such homage: Following the death of President

Franklin D. Roosevelt 18 years earlier, his likeness had been placed on a new 10-cent piece—the now long-running Roosevelt dime.

In choosing a coin for the Kennedy tribute, federal officials faced a political mine field. The Lincoln cent, Jefferson nickel and Washington quarter all had been around for at least a quarter-century, making them eligible for immediate redesign without congressional authorization. Then as now, however, government officials were reluctant to dislodge Abraham Lincoln, Thomas Jefferson and George Washington from their pedestals on the nation's regular coinage. That reluctance helps explain why these same three coins remained in production as the new millennium started—and why they may well outlast most if not all Americans now alive.

With these three coins off-limits, the only two left were the Roosevelt dime and the Franklin half dollar, both of which had made their debuts in the late 1940's and thus were well short of the statutory minimum of 25 years for replacement of a regular U.S. coin. As the only non-president appearing at the time on U.S. coinage, Benjamin Franklin proved to be the odd man out.

Congressional authorization was quickly obtained and the Mint's two top artists, Chief Engraver Gilroy Roberts and Assistant Chief Engraver Frank Gasparro, prepared the designs in less than a month so production could begin by Jan. 1, 1964. Roberts fashioned the obverse, basing his likeness of the photogenic president on the portrait he had done just three years earlier for the John F. Kennedy entry in the Mint's ongoing series of presidential medals. Gasparro crafted the reverse, which features a painstakingly intricate rendering of the U.S. presidential seal—a technical tour de force that showcased the artist's mastery of detail.

By March 1964, the Federal Reserve was distributing the first of what would turn out to be more than 433 million 1964-dated Kennedy halves. That was easily the highest one-year mintage of any U.S. half dollar up to that time. By contrast, Franklin halves never once surpassed even 100 million during a given year. Despite the record output, it wasn't enough to satisfy demand from people across the country and even around the world. Everyone wanted a Kennedy keepsake, and the handsome new half dollar—as a durable, easily obtainable memento with the U.S. government's imprimatur—quickly became the keepsake of choice. Demand for the coin gained even greater impetus from the clear artistic excellence of its design—a remarkable achievement by Roberts and Gasparro, considering how quickly they had to work.

It seems obvious in retrospect that the powers-that-be in Washington miscalculated demand for the Kennedy half dollar, evidently believing that if the Mint produced enough millions, the supply would be sufficient to force-feed it into circulation. Perhaps that would have been true—if not for the poor timing and bad luck. Barely a year after the new half dollar made its first appearance, people began hoarding older half dollars as well, for a reason having nothing to do with sentiment.

With the price of silver rising to unprecedented heights, the Treasury obtained authorization from Congress to remove or reduce the level of that metal in U.S. coinage. Beginning with coins dated 1965, the quarter and dime would no longer contain precious metal, while the half dollar's silver content would be reduced from 90 to 40 percent. The 1964 Kennedy half dollar—the first coin in the series—would prove to be the last with traditional silver content.

Almost at once, people began saving all the silver coins they could get their hands on—including the millions of Franklin and Walking Liberty half dollars then in circulation. Massive mintages of new, non-silver Washington quarters and Roosevelt dimes provided

replacements for silver coins in those series, but there were no rein-
forcements for the older half dollars that disappeared. The hoarding
of Kennedy halves continued unabated; indeed, the continued presence of silver in these coins gave people an added incentive to set
them aside, even though the precious-metal content was reduced.
The half dollar's silver content was removed altogether in 1971.

In their well-intentioned effort to provide a suitable tribute for
the nation's slain leader, Congress and the Treasury had inadvertently sounded the death knell for a useful form of coinage—one
that had served Americans well from the very earliest days of the
nation's history.

Can the half dollar be revived as a circulating coin? At this point
it seems unlikely, since Americans have learned to live without it,
simply using two quarters in its place. The Mint has continued to
make it, perhaps for no other reason than to use the denomination
in its yearly collector sets. Then again, it just may be that the Mint—
like the rest of America—feels a sentimental attachment to the coin.

▶ The Oregon Trail Half Dollar

Commemorative coinage is a fascinating segment of America's
numismatic tradition. Though all but unknown to much of the

1926 Oregon Trail half dollar. Although this is considered the most beautiful U.S. commemorative coin, it also ushered in serious abuses. *Photos
courtesy Scott A. Travers/Bowers & Merena.*

populace over the years, it has nonetheless produced some of the most interesting and historically significant coins ever issued by Uncle Sam—and, on occasion, some of the most beautiful. All of these elements are present in abundance in the Oregon Trail half dollar. So are some of the qualities that too often have tarnished the image of the series. Indeed, this exceptional coin represents at once the best and the worst of U.S. commemorative coinage.

Unlike some commemoratives whose subjects were unworthy of such a showcase, the Oregon Trail half dollar had a theme of surpassing significance: It honored the pioneers whose courage helped fulfil the nation's "Manifest Destiny."

The Oregon Trail served the same purpose for 19th century settlers as the vast Atlantic Ocean had done in earlier times for colonists venturing westward from the civilization and safety of Mother England: It beckoned them to a new way of life along a route that was filled with promise yet fraught with danger. The trail began in Missouri and meandered westward across the Great Plains, over the rugged Rockies, then northward to the unspoiled and largely unsettled Pacific Northwest. Thousands of pioneer families followed its twists and turns, setting out in Conestoga wagons and arriving months later, half a continent away, almost at the shoreline of the Pacific.

The trail's crucial role in the winning of the West clearly swayed members of Congress when authorization was sought for a coin with this theme in the mid-1920's. While turning a cold shoulder to other coin proposals, the House coinage committee approved a half dollar commemorating "the heroism of the fathers and mothers who traversed the Oregon Trail." The bill became law on May 17, 1926.

In a strictly historical sense, there was no particular impetus for the Oregon Trail half dollar— no major anniversary that it would commemorate or important celebration that it would help finance. The sponsoring organization, the Oregon Trail Memorial Association Inc., seems to have regarded it, first and foremost, not as a means of tribute but rather as a source of ongoing revenue. Ostensibly, it was planned as a means of raising funds to help set up an Oregon Trail Memorial. Plans called for selling the coin at a premium, then using the proceeds to erect appropriate monuments along the historic trail.

Its name notwithstanding, the Oregon Trail wasn't a single pathway to the West. As one historian observed, "It began anywhere, ended everywhere, and was generally undecided in between." It actually consisted of many trails—expanding in open areas, then converging in mountain passes and other constricted locations.

History books say it started in Independence, Mo., and ended in Portland, Ore., but most travelers joined it at a point along the way and many left before the final stop. Some never reached their destination: It's estimated that 20,000 bodies lie buried in unmarked graves along the trail's 2,000-mile length—victims of illness and attacks by hostile Indians.

The silver half dollar honoring the trail is itself a major landmark in U.S. coinage. Its powerful design, rich in imagery and symbolism, is the product of a felicitious collaboration between two of the nation's most gifted sculptors—James Earle Fraser and his wife, Laura Gardin Fraser. Both created other U.S. coin designs, notably James Fraser's famous Buffalo nickel design, but this may well stand as their finest achievement in the field.

On one side of the coin, an Indian faces right, his arm outstretched as if to oppose the white man's western advance. In the background is an outline map of the United States, with a line of Conestoga wagons in the nation's Northwest serving to denote the Oregon Trail. On the other side, a wagon wends westward, plodding relentlessly forward into a setting sun.

The Oregon Trail half dollar is widely regarded as the single most beautiful U.S. commemorative coin. On another level, however, it left an ugly legacy. Congress had authorized a staggering 6 million examples, six times the maximum mintage for the only other U.S. commemorative half dollar of 1926, which marked the sesquicentennial of American independence—the nation's 150th birthday. This not only demonstrated dubious judgment, but also provided an opening for mischief.

Fewer than 150,000 Oregon Trail halves were struck in 1926, or 2½ percent of the total authorization—and even at that, they didn't sell out. More than 17,000 of these were subsequently melted when sales fell off—possibly because the issue price had been doubled to $2 per coin. Undeterred, the Oregon Trail Association came back for more two years later: In 1928, it induced the Mint to strike 50,000 more examples, drawing upon the still-open authorization from Congress. This time, 44,000 ended up being melted—nearly 90 percent of the number made. Far from being the end of the "encores," the 1928 production proved to be just the beginning of a long, troubling line that would end up extending for more than a decade.

Like the trail itself, the coin appeared to ramble all over the map: It was produced in eight different years from 1926 to 1939 and at three different mints—and no fewer than 14 different examples are needed to put together a complete date-and-mint set. Congress finally slammed the door on the whole tawdry business in 1939 by suspending any further commemorative coinage for the time being. With World War II looming large, the nation had more urgent matters to deal with.

The Oregon Trail half dollar didn't travel well; its seemingly endless journey was one of the abuses that led to a halt in U.S. commemorative coinage in 1954—a hiatus that didn't end until 1982. In spite of these warts, however, this breathtaking coin is a masterpiece artistically. At the end of its long trail, it has settled into a place of well-deserved honor among the very finest U.S. coins.

❯ The 1804 Silver Dollar

Who's Number One? When it comes to rare coins, that title clearly belonged to the 1804 silver dollar as the 20th century—and second millennium—drew to a close. On the night of Aug. 30, 1999, a pristine example of this famous American rarity changed hands in a New York City auction room for $4,140,000—far and away the highest price ever paid at any public sale for any coin.

1804 Draped Bust silver dollar. Acclaimed as the "King of American Coins" and holder of the all-time price record for any coin. *Photos courtesy Scott A. Travers/Bowers & Merena.*

The sale kept the record all in the family, for the previous record holder—at $1,815,000—was yet another 1804 dollar. It isn't any wonder that this dignified-looking dollar has long been proclaimed "The King of American Coins."

For many years, mystery shrouded the origins of the 1804 dollar. Its rarity was recognized by the mid-19th century, but hobbyists were puzzled as to why it was so elusive. After all, official U.S. Mint records showed that 19,570 silver dollars had been made in 1804 at the Philadelphia Mint (the only U.S. mint in existence at the time). There were numerous theories. Some suggested the coins had been melted; others thought they might have been lost at sea. Many U.S. gold and silver coins had, in fact, been shipped abroad during the nation's formative years, and some of those are known to have ended up on the ocean floor.

The mystery was solved to most numismatists' satisfaction by Eric P. Newman and Kenneth E. Bressett in their 1962 book *The Fantastic 1804 Dollar*. After exhaustive research, the authors concluded that the 19,570 dollars listed for 1804—though struck during that year—actually carried a different date, probably 1803. It was common practice at the time to continue using dies until they wore out, even if that meant doing so in a different calendar year. This is apparent from the many early overdates. While the new date often was engraved over the old one, this didn't always occur, so it was not unusual for coins of a given date to be struck in a subsequent year with no physical evidence of this appearing on the coins.

Newman and Bressett further concluded that the first dollars dated 1804—now known to hobbyists as "original" or Class I pieces—resulted from a decision at the U.S. Treasury to include this denomination in presentation sets prepared in the mid-1830's for several Asian rulers. The U.S. government was seeking to establish trade relations with these potentates, and it was deemed desirable to help seal these bonds with suitable gifts. The objective was to include one proof specimen of each U.S. coin, and most of the coins were dated 1834, evidently reflecting the year when the sets were assembled. Since Mint records showed that silver dollars and eagles ($10 gold pieces) hadn't been made since 1804, the coins produced in those denominations were given that date for these special sets.

The 1804 dollar that set a new auction record in 1999, and the one whose record it broke, are both Class I specimens of the coin. They are among eight so-called "original" examples thought to have been struck for the presentation sets in the 1830's. There also are seven restrikes believed to have been made surreptitiously in the late 1850's by someone using old dies—perhaps a night watchman—at the Philadelphia Mint. One of these has a plain edge and is categorized as Class II, while the other six have crushed lettered edges and are said to be Class III. The Class II and Class III coins were struck from the same obverse die as the Class I examples, but a different reverse die was used.

The coin that would later sell for more than four million dollars was part of a presentation set given by U.S. envoy Edmund Roberts on Oct. 1, 1835 to the Sultan of Muscat. The fabulously wealthy sultan, sometimes referred to over the years as the "imam" of Muscat, exerted great control over coastlines along the Indian Ocean. The cased set including the silver dollar passed from the sultan's hands not long afterward. The dollar was acquired in the late 1860's by a British collector named C. A. Watters—but by then it had been removed from the set. The set had apparently been dispersed and the case had vanished. One of the other presentation sets—the King of Siam Set—does survive largely intact to this day, and is considered one of the world's greatest numismatic treasures.

The Muscat dollar hadn't changed hands since 1945, when a Vermont collector names Charles F. Childs purchased it for $5,000. It had remained in his family from then until the record-breaking 1999 sale. What sets this coin apart from all the other 1804 dollars is its breathtaking condition. Prior to the auction, the Professional Coin Grading Service (PCGS) certified it as Proof-68—a stratospheric grade level never before associated with this most famous of all U.S. coins. The previous record-holder, which came from the famous collection of Baltimore financier Louis Eliasberg Sr., was certified as Proof-63, and none of the other examples is thought to come even close to the almost unimaginable grade of the Childs specimen.

The notion of a nearly perfect 1804 dollar hit many hobbyists like a bolt from the numismatic blue when they learned of its existence shortly before the sale. Where had this "stealth superstar" been all these years, they wondered, and why hadn't they heard of it before? In point of fact, the coin had been kept under wraps by Charles Childs and his family for more than 50 years. And because its last public sale predated the development of modern grading standards by more than a generation, few had any inkling that it would be considered a "super-grade" coin when it finally re-entered the market.

"Very few people have owned this coin, and very, very few have ever handled it," said Q. David Bowers, chairman of the board of Bowers & Merena, the Wolfeboro, N.H. auction firm that sold both the Childs and Eliasberg specimens.

"All along the way, people took very good care of this coin," Bowers added. "When you think about it, it's amazing that it would stay this long in that kind of condition."

Then again, it takes an amazing coin to bring an amazing price.

▶ The Peace Dollar

Peace is an aspiration embedded just as deeply in Americans' minds and hearts as life, liberty and the pursuit of happiness. Indeed, it is the goal that underpins all the others. Yet, as the 20th century gave way to the 21st, the word "peace" had appeared on only one regular-issue U.S. coin. That coin was the Peace dollar, a silver dollar issued from 1921 to 1935—and like peace itself, its stay was brief and sporadic.

1934-S Peace dollar. The Peace dollar was the last standard silver dollar issued by the U.S. Mint. *Photos courtesy David L. Ganz.*

The Peace dollar's genesis was the Great War in Europe—a conflict recalled only later as World War I. The horrors of that conflict had left an ugly scar on America's psyche, unleashing isolationist sentiment that restrained the United States from joining the League of Nations. They also had created a hunger for lasting peace, and out of that deep desire grew the impetus for a coin that would celebrate and commemorate the restoration of peace in the wake of the bitter war.

The American Numismatic Association played a prominent role in promoting the idea of a "peace coin." One of the ANA's most energetic members, coin dealer-entrepreneur Farran Zerbe, worked tirelessly to build support for the concept. By happy coincidence, the United States Mint was confronted at the time—for purely technical reasons—with the need to start producing millions of silver dollars after a long hiatus. Under the Pittman Act of 1918, the federal government had melted more than 270 million silver dollars, mostly to aid wartime ally Great Britain, and now it was required to mint new silver dollars to replace them.

The nation had no need for new silver dollars. "Cartwheels" saw only limited use, primarily in the West, and remaining inventories were more than sufficient to serve commercial needs. Demand for the coins was so minimal, in fact, that none had been produced for more than a decade and a half, since Morgan dollars were last minted in 1904, but the Pittman Act required the Mint to make them, so it did. After a lapse of 17 years, it produced more than 86 million new Morgan dollars in 1921—the highest one-year output in the history of the series. Meanwhile, in Congress, pressure was building to authorize a silver dollar dedicated to peace. In a joint resolution, its Senate and House sponsors declared that the coin should bear "an appropriate design commemorative of the termination of the war between the Imperial German Government and the Government of the people of the United States." Congress never actually voted on the proposal, adjourning without taking action. Congressional authorization wasn't really needed, because the Morgan dollar—since it had been produced for more than the statutory minimum of 25 years—was subject to replacement without specific legislative approval. Heeding the sense of Congress, the Mint went ahead with the plan on its own.

To obtain the coin's design, a competition was held and nine distinguished artists were invited. The winner turned out to be a young Italian immigrant named Anthony de Francisci, whose portrait of Miss Liberty on the obverse of the coin bore a close—and understandable—resemblance to his wife, Teresa, herself a new American born in Italy. She had been his model—and from then until her death seven decades later, she had the distinction of being the only living person whose likeness appeared on a regular U.S. coin. The dollar's reverse shows an eagle at rest on a crag, peering toward the sun, with the word "Peace" superimposed on the rock.

The contest and start of production took place in record time: The participating artists weren't even invited until Nov. 19, 1921, yet the sketches were submitted, the winner was chosen and plaster models were readied in time to permit a limited production run before the end of the year. The Mint was able to strike barely a million examples before the year ran out, but they proved to be the finest in the series, for they were the only ones with high relief. This feature enhanced the beauty of the coins, but also represented a serious technical flaw, for it slowed production speed and made the coins impossible to stack. The Mint reduced the relief in 1922, rendering subsequent Peace dollars flatter and less detailed. The combination of low mintage and high quality make the 1921 Peace dollar one of the most coveted and valuable in the series.

By 1928, the Mint had produced enough silver dollars to satisfy the requirements of the Pittman Act. Since none had really been needed in the first place, it thereupon suspended further production. With activity winding down, the Philadelphia Mint struck just 360,649 examples in 1928, making this the lowest-mintage coin in the series. The lid on new production was tightened even more with the onset of the Depression during the following year— but like the Morgan dollar before it, the Peace dollar got a belated curtain call, appearing for the final times in 1934 and '35.

It may have been irrelevant in terms of public need, but the Peace dollar series has long held a place of honor with collectors. Although its brief life span underscores the fact that it wasn't really needed, it also makes the series more attractive in a numismatic sense—for its compact size makes it easier to complete, and completeness is a virtue highly prized by many collectors. A complete set of Peace dollars consists of just 24 date-and-mint combinations, none of them great rarities. By contrast, the Morgan series has 96 different date-and-mint varieties—four times as many—and that doesn't even include overdates and other specialized varieties. Peace dollars can be difficult to grade, and can be extremely elusive in very high levels of preservation.

The Peace dollar was the last standard U.S. silver dollar struck for circulation—the last dollar coin with the traditional alloy of 90-percent silver and 10-percent copper. In that respect this coin, issued to mark the end of the "war to end all wars," was itself the silver dollar that ended all silver dollars in the United States.

▶ The Saint-Gaudens Double Eagle

If a beauty contest were held to rate the artistic merits of all United States coins, the almost certain winner would be the stunning double eagle (or $20 gold piece) designed by renowned sculptor Augustus Saint-Gaudens. In his fascinating book *Numismatic Art in America,* Cornelius Vermeule, longtime curator of the Boston Museum of Fine Arts, described this masterpiece as "perhaps the most majestic coin ever to bear our national imprint"—and few connoisseurs of U.S. coinage art would disagree.

1907 ultra-high-relief Saint-Gaudens double eagle. The very first, and very best, example of this stunning U.S. gold coin. *Photos courtesy Scott A. Travers/Bowers & Merena.*

The "Saint," as collectors call it, was one of two U.S. gold coins that resulted from a covenant between Saint-Gaudens and the nation's 26th president, Theodore Roosevelt. "TR" was undoubtedly the most dynamic leader ever to occupy the White House; during the seven and a half years of his presidency, he used his "bully pulpit" to pursue an agenda crammed with major projects: He battled big business, pressed for construction of the Panama Canal, mediated an end to the Russo-Japanese War (winning the Nobel Peace Prize for his efforts) and fought for conservation of America's natural resources.

While juggling these initiatives, and numerous others as well, Roosevelt found time to set in motion a process he liked to describe as his "pet crime"—a massive redesign of U.S. coinage. He believed, with good reason, that the nation's coinage art had grown stagnant and needed a face lift. His feet were firmly planted in the new 20th century, and he wanted U.S. coins to be fresh and forward-looking, not pale reflections of the past. The gold coinage, in particular, had been virtually unchanged since the first half of the 1800's (except for the winnowing out of several denominations that were no longer issued).

This project had been in the back of Roosevelt's fertile mind since the time he took office in September 1901, following the assassination of his predecessor, William McKinley. It didn't come to the forefront until 1905, when the president chose Saint-Gaudens to design the inaugural medal marking the start of his second and final term. Roosevelt was delighted with the medal (widely considered the finest inaugural medal in U.S. history)—and when the men met later at a Washington dinner party, he prevailed upon the artist to serve as an accessory to his "crime."

Saint-Gaudens had nothing to prove; at the age of 56, he had long since established himself as America's foremost sculptor. The president's grand vision, however, fanned the creative fires still burning deep inside him, and he went home from Washington determined to meet the challenge by reshaping U.S. coinage in the image of magnificent ancient models.

Both men greatly admired the high-relief coinage of ancient Greece, and Roosevelt asked Saint-Gaudens to create a complete series of U.S. coin designs springing from those classical antecedents. The artist chose to start by preparing new designs for the two largest U.S. gold coins, the Liberty double eagle and Coronet eagle ($20 and $10 gold pieces, respectively), both of which had borne the same basic designs for more than half a century. Saint-Gaudens' health was failing, but his genius remained vibrant. Both coins turned out to be masterworks of numismatic art—with the double eagle, especially, soaring to artistic heights never attained before or since by any other U.S. coin. Sadly, they were to be their creator's last works, for he died in 1907, just before their release.

The double eagle's obverse features a full-length portrait of a female figure symbolizing Liberty—a torch held in her right hand and an olive branch in her left—shown in full stride with the sun's rays behind her. "Liberty" is inscribed above her and the U.S. Capitol Building appears in the background to the left of her flowing gown. She is encircled by 46 stars—one for each state in the

Union at that time (two more were added in 1912, when New Mexico and Arizona brought the number of states to 48). The coin's reverse depicts a soaring eagle—perhaps the most spectacular likeness of this lordly bird ever to appear on a U.S. coin. Below the eagle is the sun, with its rays extended upward. Above it, in two semicircular tiers, are the mandatory inscription "United States of America" and the statement of value, "Twenty Dollars."

To help give the coin a clean, uncluttered look, Saint-Gaudens placed one other required motto, "E Pluribus Unum," along the edge, where it would not detract from his powerful images. He and Roosevelt conspired to omit the motto "In God We Trust," but members of Congress detected the omission and legislated its presence on all new double eagles starting partway through production in 1908, the coin's second year of issue.

On orders from the president, the Mint struck a handful of exquisite proof specimens with extremely high—or "ultra-high"—relief prior to the start of regular coin production in 1907. These included a single piece with a plain edge and about two dozen others with "E Pluribus Unum" on the edge. The edges of these coins are roughly twice as thick as those on the standard specimens eventually struck for circulation. The design details are incredibly sharp—not surprisingly, considering that each received nine blows from the dies at a pressure of 172 tons. The date on the ultra-high-relief specimens is shown in Roman numerals as MCMVII, a feature meant by Saint-Gaudens to reinforce the coins' classical look. Preeminent numismatic researcher Walter Breen once commented, in discussing these very first "Saints," that "only these faithfully represent Saint-Gaudens' conception, cherished as the stunning climax of American coin design."

Standard-relief Saint-Gaudens double eagles were issued sporadically until 1933, when the nation abandoned gold coinage. The U.S. Mint produced nearly half a million examples dated 1933, but the Treasury has long maintained that these were never released prior to the Gold Surrender Order promulgated that year by another President Roosevelt—Theodore Roosevelt's cousin Franklin D. Almost all of these were melted, but a few survived and one, purchased with Mint approval by Egypt's King Farouk during the 1940's, was scheduled to come up for sale—with the federal government's blessing—in 2002. It was widely expected to shatter the existing price record for any single coin, possibly bringing as much as $10 million. That would get the new millennium off to a flying start, and add some extra luster to the King of Hobbies' crown.

A Glossary of Numismatic Terms

Assay—A test of coins selected at random to determine whether they conform with predetermined standards of weight and fineness. For many years, an Assay Commission including public members met each year at the Philadelphia Mint to examine samples of U.S. coinage from the previous year. The tradition became largely symbolic after precious metal was removed from U.S. coinage, and President Jimmy Carter discontinued the practice in 1977.

Bullion Coin—A coin with high precious-metal content that is issued primarily to be saved as a store of value, rather than spent as money. The United States produces bullion coins known as American Eagles in gold, silver and platinum. These are sold to the public at modest premiums over the market value of the bullion they contain.

Civil War Tokens—Base-metal pieces issued privately during the Civil War to serve as coinage substitutes. These came in two major varieties—"patriotic tokens" with war-related themes and "store cards" distributed by merchants to advertise their wares and provide their customers with a medium of exchange.

Commemorative—A special coin issued to honor some person, place or event, usually on a major anniversary and in a form not meant for circulation but only for sale to collectors at a premium.

Devices—The designs and inscriptions that are on a coin. On the vast majority of U.S. coins, these are the raised areas. There are two notable exceptions: The $2½ and $5 Indian Head gold coins of 1908–1929 had these elements incused, or sunken below the surface.

Die—A hardened metal punch used to impart the design to one side of a coin blank. The die carries the design in mirror image to the way it will appear on the coin itself.

Electrum—A naturally occurring mixture of gold and silver that was used in ancient Lydia to strike the world's earliest known coins.

Exergue—A space below the main design of a coin and separated from it by a line. On many coins, this is the location of the date.

Exonumia—A term used to describe tokens, medals and other objects that resemble coins, and are widely collected by coin hobbyists, but normally do not function as money.

Fields—The flat parts of a coin's surface that are around and between the raised elements that make up the design. On proof coins, these are generally polished to a brilliant, mirror-like finish.

Fineness—A term describing the precious-metal content of a gold or silver coin (or one made of some other precious metal, such as platinum). For most of U.S. coinage history, circulating gold and silver coins had a fineness of .900, or 90 percent.

Flan—A term describing a coin blank; also known as a *planchet*.

Fractional Currency—Paper money issued in denominations of less than a dollar. The United States issued large quantities of such notes during and after the Civil War to serve as replacements for coins, which were being widely hoarded at the time. The public scorned these notes as "shinplasters," but they are now highly sought after as collectibles.

Frosted—An adjective describing the dull but highly attractive appearance of raised areas on proof coins. These stand out because of their contrast with the bright, mirrorlike finish of the background.

Grading—A system that measures the degree of wear—or lack of wear—on a given coin. It takes into account any defects or damage the coin may have suffered, as well as positive attributes such as bright luster and attractive toning.

Hammered Coin—A coin produced by placing a blank between two dies, then striking one die with a hammer to force them together.

Hub—A piece of steel used to produce a die. On a hub, a coin's design appears as it will on the coin itself. On a die, the design appears in a mirror image. Typically, a die is struck more than once while it is receiving the image from a hub. If the alignment shifts between these "hubbings," coins struck with that die will bear a doubled image. That's what happened with some Lincoln cents in 1955, 1972 and 1995.

Legal Tender—A term used to signify that coins or paper money are redeemable by the government at face value.

Lettered Edge—A feature whereby an inscription is placed on the edge of a coin. Many early U.S. coins—including even the pure copper "large cent" and half cent—had edge lettering denoting their value as money.

Limited Edition—A coin issue whose mintage is restricted to a number announced in advance, or to a number for which orders are received by a given deadline.

Matte—A dull finish applied to a coin—usually a proof—by a mint.

Milled Coin—A coin produced mechanically, rather than by hand—originally on a screw press powered by a horse-drawn machine called a "mill." Milled coins are superior in quality to the hammered coins they replaced around the 16th century.

Mint—The building where coins are manufactured; or, in general terms, the agency that oversees coin production. Since the start of U.S. coinage in 1792, the nation's main mint has been located in Philadelphia. As of 2002, there also were three branch mints—in Denver, San Francisco and West Point, N.Y.

Mint Mark—A letter (or letters), symbol or some other marking placed upon a coin to designate the mint where it was produced. On U.S. coins, mint marks take the form of letters. Coins produced at the Denver Mint, for example, carry a "D" mint mark, while those made in San Francisco bear an "S." Throughout most of U.S. coinage history, coins struck at the main mint in Philadelphia had no mint mark; in recent years, however, a "P" has been placed on all coins from that mint except the cent.

Mint State—A term describing the condition of a high-quality business-strike coin that has never entered circulation and therefore has no wear. Unlike a *proof*, a mint-state coin is struck with normal dies, a regular coin blank is used and the blank is normally struck only once. As a result, the coin does not have the same mirrorlike finish and exquisite detail as a proof. Nonetheless, its pristine condition makes it highly desirable to collectors.

Mirror Finish—The shiny, flawless surface imparted to brilliant proof coins through the use of a special blank and special dies, as well as more painstaking production techniques. In producing such coins, Mint technicians polish the blanks and the dies.

Motto—An inscription stamped on a coin, such as "Liberty," "E Pluribus Unum" or "In God We Trust."

Mule—A mint error on which the "heads" side of one coin is mated with the "tails" side of a different coin. In 2000, the U.S. Mint produced a small number of mules combining the obverse of a statehood Washington quarter with the reverse of a Sacagawea "golden dollar." These were struck on coin blanks meant for the dollar coin.

Notgeld—A term applied to emergency money—particularly the all but worthless paper money issued by Germany following World War I.

Numismatics—The science, study or collecting of coins and related items, such as paper money, medals, tokens, orders and decorations and similar objects. A person who engages in such pursuits is called a *numismatist*.

Obverse—The "heads" side of a coin—the one that carries the principal design or device, and usually the date. In the case of British and Canadian coins, the obverse is the side that depicts the monarch.

Pattern—An experimental coin produced to showcase a new design, metal, size or denomination that is under consideration by the government. The United States Mint produced many patterns in the second half of the 19th century, but relatively few since that time. Most surviving patterns are extremely rare—but because there are relatively few collectors pursuing such material, they bring much smaller premiums than regular-issue coins of comparable rarity.

Planchet—A piece of metal the size of a coin before the design is stamped on it; also known as a *flan* or a *coin blank*.

Proof—A coin struck with special equipment and techniques, on a carefully selected and polished blank, in order to bring out every detail of the design and impart a mirrorlike appearance to the field or background area. On modern coins, the raised areas—the designs and lettering—generally are frosted, and this contrasts appealingly with the brilliant background. The coins are struck twice or more in order to provide even greater sharpness of detail. Typically, proofs are struck only for presentation or for sale at a premium as collectibles.

Reeding—Small, raised parallel lines that are on the edge of a coin, originally used to protect against the filing of gold and silver shavings from precious-metal coins.

Relief—The height of a coin's design above its surface. Raised portions that help determine this level include the designs and inscriptions.

Restrike—A coin produced from original dies but at a later date.

Reverse—The back or "tails" side of a coin; the opposite of the *obverse*.

Set—Two or more coins that share common characteristics, usually from the same time period. The United States Mint issues annual proof sets and uncirculated coin sets (better known to hobbyists as "mint sets").

Uncirculated—The condition of a coin that has never entered circulation. By definition, an *uncirculated* coin can have no wear that is traceable to use in commerce. However, because of the mass production methods and bulk bagging used with modern coins, a coin can have scratches, dents or other imperfections and still be considered uncirculated—provided that these can be shown to be mint-related.

Books for Further Reading

Grading Guides

American Numismatic Association: Edited by Ken Bressett and A. Kosoff; introduction by Q. David Bowers. *Official American Numismatic Association Grading Standards for United States Coins.* Fifth Edition. Colorado Springs, Colo., ANA, 1996.

> *The ANA grading guide originally used line drawings of coins to illustrate grading differences. It now uses photographs, which are a big improvement. Like the grading service the ANA formerly operated (but since has sold), however, this guide is more of an academic exercise than a market-oriented presentation. It is interesting and informative on a technical level, but less so in a practical vein.*

Brown, Martin R. and John W. Dunn. *A Guide to the Grading of United States Coins.* Seventh Edition. Denison, General Distributors, 1980.

> *The "Brown and Dunn book" has been around since 1959, but has steadily lost relevance to the marketplace it initially was meant to serve. This is reflected in the fact that it has not been revised since 1980. The book uses drawings, rather than photographs, which has been one of its major shortcomings from the very start. It's a worthwhile book for collectors to keep on their shelves for historical reference, but not much use on a bourse floor.*

Halperin, James L; Introduction by Scott A. Travers. *How to Grade U.S. Coins.* Dallas, Ivy Press, 1990

This book incorporates much of the material that previously appeared in The NCI Grading Guide, *which served as a guide to the standards of the Numismatic Certification Institute, an early grading service known for relatively loose standards. That association carries somewhat of a stigma, but this volume offers a number of worthwhile innovations, notably the use of colorized coin "maps" to highlight grade-sensitive areas on various coins.*

Professional Coin Grading Service: Edited by Scott A. Travers; John W. Dannreuther, text author; introduction by Q. David Bowers. *The Official Guide to Coin Grading and Counterfeit Detection.* New York, House of Collectibles/Random House, 1997.

This is the most comprehensive grading guide available, and the most authoritative. It was prepared under the aegis of the leading coin grading service, PCGS, and written and edited by two of the greatest authorities in the field, John Dannreuther and Scott Travers. It not only provides extensive information on grading itself but also offers intriguing insights into the operation of a top grading service. I had a role in this book as its numismatic editor.

Ruddy, James F. *Photograde: A Photographic Grading Encyclopedia for United States Coins.* Eighteenth Edition. Wolfeboro, N.H., Bowers & Merena Galleries, 1990.

When it first appeared in the early 1970's, Photograde *was a major step forward in the systematizing of coin grading. Its use of photos, rather than drawings, simplified grading for readers. In the intervening years, the grading of mint-state coins has become too complex for such a basic approach, but the book remains a helpful reference aid in the grading of circulated coins, where nuances are less significant.*

Annual Price Guides

Editors of *Coin World, Coin World Guide to U.S. Coins, Prices and Value Trends.* Fifteenth Edition. Sidney, Ohio, Amos Press, 2002.

This book is an annual compilation of the prices listed weekly in the popular Trends *section of* Coin World, *the coin industry's largest-circulation*

*newspaper. These listings are accompanied by price-performance charts
that serve as valuable gauges of how the market is doing on a series-by-
series basis.*

Travers, Scott A. *The Insider's Guide to U.S. Coin Values.* Tenth Edition.
New York, Dell Publishing/Random House, 2001.
   *Unlike other price guides, this book provides detailed valuations, based on
   actual transactions, for coins in the mint-state range—including rare-date
   coins normally not charted in such books. Mintage information is unusually accurate and up-to-date because of the involvement of noted numismatic researcher R. W. Julian.*

Yeoman, R. S. Edited by Kenneth Bressett. *A Guide Book of United States
   Coins.* Fifty-fifth Edition. New York, St. Martin's Press, 2001.
Yeoman, R. S. Edited by Kenneth Bressett. *Handbook of United States
   Coins.* Fifty-ninth Edition. New York, St. Martin's Press, 2001.
   The Guide Book, *familiarly known as the "Red Book" because of its
   cover color, lists retail prices—those that buyers should expect to pay dealers for coins. The* Handbook, *or "Blue Book," lists wholesale prices—
   those that dealers would pay to buy coins from collectors. Both books have
   been in print for more than 50 years and both have become collectibles in
   their own right. They no longer serve as day-to-day market tools, as they
   once did, but they remain important sources of historical information and
   general guides to values.*

General Interest

Akers, David W. *A Handbook of 20th Century United States Gold Coins,
   1907–1933.* Wolfeboro, N.H., Bowers & Merena Galleries, 1988.
Alexander, David T., editor. *Coin World Comprehensive Catalog and Ency-
   clopedia of United States Coins.* Second Edition. Sidney, Ohio. Amos
   Press, 1998.
Bowers, Q. David. *A Buyer's and Enthusiast's Guide to Flying Eagle and
   Indian Cents.* Wolfeboro, N.H, Bowers & Merena Galleries, 1996.
Bowers, Q. David. *American Numismatics Before the Civil War 1760–1860.*
   Wolfeboro, N.H., Bowers & Merena Galleries, 1998.

Bowers, Q. David. *Commemorative Coins of the United States: A Complete Encyclopedia*. Wolfeboro, N.H., Bowers & Merena Galleries, 1991.

Bowers, Q. David. *The History of United States Coinage as Illustrated by the Garrett Collection*. Los Angeles, Bowers & Ruddy Galleries, 1979.

Bowers, Q. David. *Silver Dollars and Trade Dollars of the United States: A Complete Encyclopedia*. Wolfeboro, N.H., Bowers & Merena Galleries, 1993.

Bowers, Q. David. *United States Gold Coins: An Illustrated History*. Los Angeles, Bowers & Ruddy Galleries, 1982.

Breen, Walter. *Walter Breen's Complete Encyclopedia of U.S. and Colonial Coins*. New York, Doubleday, 1988.

Breen, Walter. *Walter Breen's Encyclopedia of U.S. and Colonial Proof Coins, 1722–1989*. Second Edition. Wolfeboro, N.H., Bowers & Merena Galleries, 1989.

Breen, Walter. Edited by Mark Borckardt. *Walter Breen's Encyclopedia of Early United States Cents, 1793–1814*. Wolfeboro, N.H., Bowers & Merena Galleries, 2000.

Breen, Walter. *Walter Breen's Encyclopedia of United States Half Cents, 1793–1857*. South Gate, American Institute of Numismatic Research, 1983.

Bressett, Kenneth E. *The Official Whitman Statehood Quarters Collector's Handbook*. New York, St. Martin's Press, 2000.

Bressett, Kenneth E. *The Whitman Guide to Coin Collecting*. New York, St. Martin's Press, 1999.

Crosby, Sylvester S. Introduction by Eric P. Newman. *The Early Coins of America*. Lawrence, Quarterman Publications, 1983.

Doty, Richard. *America's Money, America's Story*. Iola, Wis., Krause Publications, 1998.

Friedberg, Robert. Edited by Ira S. and Arthur Friedberg. *Paper Money of the United States*. Fifteenth Edition. Clifton, N.J., Coin and Currency Institute, 1999.

Fivaz, Bill and J. T. Stanton. Edited by Mike Ellis. *The Cherrypicker's Guide to Rare Die Varieties*. Fourth Edition. Savannah, Ga., Stanton Books & Supplies, 2000.

Ganz, David L. *The Official Guidebook to America's State Quarters.* New York, House of Collectibles/Random House, 2000.

Ganz, David L. *Official Guide to U.S. Commemorative Coins.* Chicago, Bonus Books, 1999.

Ganz, David L. "Value of Coin Collection." Rochester, N.Y., Lawyers Cooperative Publishing, 1989. Originally published as: *American Jurisprudence, Proof of Facts. 3rd Series,* volume 5.

Herbert, Alan. *The Official Identification and Price Guide to Minting Varieties and Errors.* Fifth Edition. New York, House of Collectibles/Random House, 1991.

Highfill, John W. *The Comprehensive U.S. Silver Dollar Encyclopedia.* Broken Arrow, Okla., Highfill Press, 1992.

Hessler, Gene. *Comprehensive Catalog of U.S. Paper Money.* Sixth Edition. Port Clinton, Ohio, BNR Press, 1997.

Hoberman, Gerald. *The Art of Coins and Their Photography.* London, Spink & Son, 1981.

Judd, J. Hewitt. *United States Pattern, Experimental and Trial Pieces.* Seventh Edition. Racine, Wis., Western Publishing, 1982.

Kagin, Donald H. *Private Gold Coins and Patterns of the United States.* New York, Arco, 1981.

Krause, Chester L. and Robert F. Lemke. *Standard Catalog of U.S. Paper Money.* Twentieth Edition. Iola, Wis., Krause Publications, 2001.

Krause, Chester L. and Clifford L. Mishler. *Standard Catalog of World Coins.* Twenty-ninth Edition. Iola, Wis., Krause Publications, 2001.

Lange, David W. *The Complete Guide to Lincoln Cents.* Wolfeboro, N.H., Bowers & Merena Galleries, 1996.

Logan, Russell J. and John W. McCloskey. *Federal Half Dimes 1792–1837.* Manchester, N.H., John Reich Collectors Society, 1998.

Margolis, Arnold. *The Error Coin Encyclopedia.* Third Edition. New York, Margolis, 2000.

Mossman, Philip L. *Money of the American Colonies and Confederation.* New York, American Numismatic Society, 1993.

Pollock, Andrew W. III. *United States Patterns and Related Issues.* Wolfeboro, N.H., Bowers & Merena Galleries, 1994.

Reiver, Jules. *United States Early Silver Dollars, 1794–1803,* Iola, Wis., Krause Publications, 1999.

Rochette, Edward C. *The Other Side of the Coin.* Frederick, Colo., Renaissance House, 1985.

Sheldon, William H. With the collaboration of Dorothy I. Paschal and Walter Breen; introduction by Denis W. Loring. *Penny Whimsy.* New York, Durst, 1990.

Swiatek, Anthony J. *Commemorative Coins of the United States.* Second Edition. Sidney, Ohio, Coin World, 2001.

Taxay, Don. *An Illustrated History of U.S. Commemorative Coinage.* New York, Arco Publishing, 1967.

Taxay, Don. Introduction by John J. Ford Jr. *Counterfeit, Misstruck and Unofficial U.S. Coins.* New York, Arco Publishing, 1963.

Taxay, Don. Foreword by Gilroy Roberts. *The U.S. Mint and Coinage: An Illustrated History From 1776 to the Present.* New York, Arco Publishing, 1966.

Travers, Scott A. *The Coin Collector's Survival Manual.* Fourth Edition. Chicago, Bonus Books, 2000.

Travers, Scott A. *How to Make Money in Coins Right Now.* Second Edition. New York, House of Collectibles/Random House, 2001.

Travers, Scott A. *One-Minute Coin Expert—Find a Fortune in Your Pocket Change.* Fourth Edition. New York, House of Collectibles/Random House, 2001.

Travers, Scott A. Foreword by Q. David Bowers; introduction by Ed Reiter. *Scott Travers' Top 88 Coins Over $100.* Chicago, Bonus Books, 1998.

Vagi, David L. *Coinage and History of the Roman Empire, c. 82 B.C.–A.D. 480.* Sidney, Ohio, Coin World/Amos Press, 1999.

Van Allen, Leroy C. *Comprehensive Catalog and Encyclopedia of Morgan and Peace Dollars.* Fourth Edition. Orlando, Fla., Worldwide Ventures, 1998.

Van Ryzin, Robert R. *Crime of 1873—The Comstock Connection.* Iola, Wis., Krause Publications, 2001.

Vermeule, Cornelius Clarkson. *Numismatic Art in America.* Cambridge, Mass., Belknap Press/Harvard University Press, 1971.

Winter, Douglas. *Charlotte Mint Gold Coins, 1838–1861.* Wolfeboro, N.H., Bowers & Merena Galleries, 1987.

Winter, Douglas. *Gold Coins of the Old West, the Carson City Mint, 1870–1893*. Wolfeboro, N.H., Bowers & Merena Galleries, 1994.

Winter, Douglas. *New Orleans Mint Gold Coins, 1839–1909*. Wolfeboro, N.H., Bowers & Merena Galleries, 1992.

Index